THE PENNY PINCHER'S BOOK

THE PENNY PINCHER'S BOOK

Easy Ways of Living Better for Less

John and Irma Mustoe

SOUVENIR PRESS

First published 1995 by Souvenir Press Ltd,
43 Great Russell Street, London WC1B 3PA
and simultaneously in Canada

ISBN 0 285 63285 X

Printed in Great Britain by
the Guernsey Press Company Ltd, Guernsey, Channel Islands.

CONTENTS

1 The Basics 9

2 Shopping 37

3 DIY 47

4 Recycling 77

5 Gardening 91

6 Transport 105

7 Appliances 117

8 Food 129

9 Clothes 149

10 Make-up and Grooming 163

   Index 175

In this book you will find hundreds of ways of saving money. Some of the ideas can save you hundreds of pounds a year, others just a few pounds. Some ideas are rather fun, others a bit laborious for the savings made. The whole book can be read on this level, and you can choose out of it ideas that are relevant to your life.

Underneath what we hope are a lot of good ideas there is another big idea: how to make life more satisfying.

In our life together we have had long periods when we were making good money, working hard, and having a miserable time. We could not afford the holiday for the children that would have meant so much to them. We were sick with worry over the mortgage payments. Our bank would write us letters beginning 'We thought you would like to know that your overdraft has reached . . .' when of course we did not want to know anything of the kind.

In other years our joint income was very low. Some years our little company ran at a loss. Those were not good times either, but they were not significantly worse than when we were earning big money.

We looked around us, and our experience seemed to be common. Some low-income people are happy and some high-income people are in despair. Some people on low incomes are sunk in misery and some people on high incomes are full of joy.

Maybe, we thought, it is not how much money we earn that is crucial, but how much we spend relative to the amount we earn. Mr Micawber, Dickens' character in *David Copperfield*, was not the first or last to find that if expenditure exceeds income, even by a little, then misery is the result. That's when we started publishing *The Penny Pincher Paper:* the response has been overwhelming.

The first thing that penny pinchers try to achieve is to cut down slightly on their expenditure, so that income covers outgoings. Now money is not a black cloud over our heads, but is just one of those things that we use to give quality to our lives.

Money is treated as an essential, but not ruling, factor in the life of a penny pincher. A dozen small economies and a lot of planning give control. Now money can be spent to give us greater satisfaction.

Spending money must be a skill at least as important as earning it. Making things last has got to be equal to buying something new. There is more satisfaction to be had from making your own than in making do with something produced in a factory.

Read on. Learn to make and to mend, and to do without. With the money saved there are choices before you. If you can then afford it, buy a cottage in Normandy, learn Italian, take the children camping in Scotland, start an environmental group, or even put the stuff into savings. They are all good choices. They are all choices for you to make.

Have fun with your money!

The Penny Pincher Paper is available on subscription or in single copies from: The Penny Pincher Paper, Thurleigh, Bedfordshire, MK44 2EE.

1
THE BASICS

**A little about budgeting,
and everyday things anybody can do**

Refrigerate candles for a few hours before using and they will burn more slowly, drip less, and give you better value for your money.

Kitchen foil is washable — again and again and again. Say goodbye to it, though, if it has been used for meat products, especially poultry.

Cut out one cup of coffee or tea per day for one month. You will probably save over £1.

Rescue a dried-out loaf of bread by dipping it into water and warming in the oven WHILE SOMETHING ELSE IS BAKING. If you have to heat up the whole oven just for the sake of one stale loaf of bread it's not penny-pinching, it's experimenting.

Instant coffee jars make excellent storage jars for foods. You can decorate them if you feel so compelled.

Roll a lemon, or other citrus fruit, with your hands, back and forth on the worktop surface, before squeezing it and you will get more juice. You can also heat the lemon to get more juice, but that means paying for the heat, so warm the lemon and yourself with the exercise — it's free.

Use rubber tap extensions on your sink taps — don't smash china.

Pack a lunch instead of eating out — and for the same amount of money that you would spend on lunch, you can pack a gourmet feast.

Pour olive oil into a pepper shaker so that you sprinkle it onto pizza, salads and so on, rather than glug it.

Buy smaller-sized eggs.

Scrape every bit of butter or margarine from the wrapper. Such a lovely parsimonious feeling.

It is actually cheaper to cook double amounts of a casserole and freeze half than it is to cook one casserole and then another one later.

Water is a wonderful extender, much used by food manufacturers and by the makers of household goods; you can do it, too. Add to washing-up liquid. Add to yeast extract. Add to milk. Add to juices.

For almost-free warm water, keep a kettle on the gas pilot light.

If you use a scouring powder which comes in a tin with sticky tape over the dispensing holes, just remove part of the tape. You know you use too much of the stuff, anyway. Everybody else does.

Never mind the cornflakes — just look at the packaging!

If you have inadvertently bought packaged cereals, make sure you get your money's worth by using the packaging, which is MUCH more valuable. Did you know that in scientific tests, rats that were fed the cereals were poorly nourished; those that were fed the packaging alone fared better. Surely you can learn from a rat?

Cereal boxes can be used as file-holders. You can cut off the top, trim the sides down at an angle, or use them turned sideways to hold files.

Cereal boxes — especially the ones with white inners — can also be cut apart and used as postcards.

The bags inside cereal boxes are wonderful. Why don't bread manufactures use them instead of the polythene sort? Probably because they make the bread last longer?

Cereal bags are superb for the freezer. Wash them and use them again. And again (always with the exception of poultry products).

Wash cereal bags and other food bags — but don't use so much washing-up liquid that it would be cheaper to buy another bag! A couple of drops suffice.

Upturn those sauce bottles. You paid for all the contents . . . get all the contents out.

Write small.

Faxing messages after six in the evening can be much cheaper than posting.

Seventeen first-class stamps = £4.25. Seventeen second-class stamps = £3.23.

Junk mail isn't ALL junk. In fact it is so useful, one should request to receive it rather than the other way round. Before you mutter and throw it away, look through it to see if there is something useful that you can use. If it has been printed on one side only, there is a free sheet of paper on the other side. You can use that for writing on, or you can make your own envelopes if you like. Speaking of envelopes, there are often return envelopes in junk mail — you can either cross through the address and the postpaid bit, or paste on a label from your favourite charity, or take the envelope carefully apart and turn it inside out, regluing it along the same edges as before. Often junk mail uses very expensive card or paper, so take advantage of the quality.

Clear out those unwanted photographs — but use them as postcards instead of throwing them away.

Old cutlery trays organise spools of thread, zips, buttons, sewing tools.

Oranges can be stuck with cloves to make a long-lasting pomander for the wardrobe.

If you work in an office, change your clothes when you get home instead of keeping on good ones. Hang up the clothes you've worn all day so that they air and drop out a lot of the wrinkles of life.

Steam-iron woollen clothes during winter to kill moth eggs. It's the larvae, not the flying moths, that do the damage. Smells better than pongy mothballs, too! *More on page 158.*

At jumble/car boot/attic sales and charity shops, you may not like the fashions on show, but consider the buttons!

Clean suede with art gum or plastic erasers.

Take the trouble to bind sheet corners and reinforce towel edges, preferably before they become frayed.

Ice cube trays keep earrings and other similar fiddly little things in organised groups.

Put empty scent bottles or talcum boxes into drawers to extend their useful life.

Never, repeat never, buy special paper for lining drawers. Use leftover wallpaper or go and buy a roll of 'lining paper' meant for walls. Even better is washable paper.

Save another pound: buy a pair of 99p tights instead of £1.99 ones.

Babies are expensive. Yes or no?

Well, yes, actually, even if you do have generous friends-and-relations who pass on clothes and so on, but if we all waited until we could afford to have a family, we probably wouldn't have one. Still, we don't have to spend on them as though there were no tomorrow — quite the opposite, because you should be teaching them from childhood that one should be thrifty. Don't let children dictate to you what you should purchase. Be gentle if you wish, but establish very early on that you do not buy ANYTHING just because 'all the other kids have it . . .' You may feel like a rat at the time, but believe me, you will have your reward when they come to you as young adults and say, 'I'm so glad you brought me up as you did.'

Newborn babies don't need lots of 'newborn' sized clothes — they only fit for ten days.

Babies' clothes sized three months do not fit for three months.

They may be old-fashioned, but cloth nappies are still the best choice for economy — better for your wallet, and for babies, and ultimately for all of us, considering the waste problem and health hazards when dumped.

Use bicarbonate of soda as a deodorant (but note that it is not an antiperspirant): wash with warm soap and water, sprinkle a little (about half a teaspoon is generous) on your damp face cloth, apply. It works. Bicarbonate of soda has an absolute multitude of uses! One of the best deodorants ever, nonallergenic, cheaper, a superb cleaning material . . . what more does one want?

Toothpaste is not one of life's necessities. Brush your teeth with bicarbonate of soda, or half-soda/half-salt.

If you do use toothpaste, don't squueze it the entire length of the toothbrush! This is a fallacy perpetuated by the toothpaste manufacturers and advertising departments! When have you ever seen an ad with a small amount of toothpaste on the brush? Cut back by half or more.

Get out the last little bit of shampoo, roll-on, make-up, etc. Turn bottles on end until truly empty. This simple method will get virtually everything out, but then you can cut tubes open and scoop out any lingering bits lurking in corners.

Dilute shampoo by a third and it will not only last longer but will give a much better lather.

Dry razor blades after using and they will last much longer. Not an old wives' tale, but old soldiers will know: officers in World War I used to carry not one, but seven cut-throat razors in a folding bag, using one each day so that the following week the steel had 'unbent' to its original sharp edge. And you can still do it, even with so-called throw-away blades.

Buy a bottle of washing-up liquid instead of shampoo.

17

Buy a 'copy perfume' at a market stall — they are quite good!

Buy make-up from the half-price basket.

Lipbrushes get out the last memory of lipstick from tubes.

Store new bars of soap in the airing cupboard to make them hard. They last longer. Soft soaps dissolve too quickly.

Plant lettuce seeds! A packet costs about 75p. Cost of a single lettuce in shops: 40-80p each. A 15g packet of seeds produces about 2,000 lettuces.

If you've inadvertently boiled too much water in the kettle, use the surplus to pour over your most despised weed. Makes you feel so much better about boiling too much in the first place, and it's superior to any chemical!

Walk a mile instead of driving — not only will you save pennies, but you will feel better.

Use no petrol at all for one day.

Cut down your speed from 70 mph to 60 mph for a petrol saving of about 15 per cent.

Wash your own car instead of using a car wash.

Share a ride to work.

Keep a place in the freezer for orange and lemon bits — save peels when you've used just the juice, and the pulp (for its juice later) when you've grated the peel for a recipe.

Keep sliced bread in the freezer. It thaws in seconds, so take out only what you need.

Polythene bags are washable. Throw them away, however, if meat has been stored in them.

Don't forget that it's cheaper to phone friends and relations after six o'clock and at weekends than it is during weekday hours.

If you make long-distance calls, you should have Mercury. It costs pennies a month — less than a pound a month — and the savings are impressive. The itemised bills will concentrate your attention even further. Wonderful.

Keep your cooker clean — even if just for efficiency! Don't make it work just to heat encrusted crud.

Use only as much washing powder as you really need depending on the softness of your water.

Scrape out the lingering wash powder on the box seams. It's another of those activities which, although it won't save you a fortune, gives a warm glow of THRIFT.

If you iron towels and underwear you are certifiable.

COLD? Before you reach for that thermostat, PUT ON A SWEATER! It's paid for—the heat isn't.

Still cold? Then DO something — vacuum, dust, make up a bed, wash a window, get some exercise somehow, and you will not only feel warm, but you will feel better.

Rinse your hands in cold water. Sounds awful? Then think about it: you probably already do, but you do it under the HOT tap, turning it off before you get hot water. But you have wasted the hot water that was drawn from the cylinder and which will then go cold in the pipes while the heater works to heat up the new cold water which refilled the cylinder.

Two or even three lightweight sweaters are warmer than one thick sweater.

Two pairs of tights (or socks if you're a chap) are much, much warmer than one.

More for the girls: keep your winter skirts long — mini skirts make maxi thighs!

If you're sitting still, wrap an afghan or small blanket around your shoulders. If you are writing, or something similar, you will find that fingerless gloves are wonderfully warm.

At night, keep warm by wearing bedsocks — and remember all the old pictures of people wearing nightcaps? You lose more heat from the top of your head than anywhere else.

Sleep with wool underneath you — a fleece if you have it, or you could use an old felted sweater.

Close doors to rooms that you don't use — keep them cool. Keep the heat where it's needed.

Close the curtains at night to help keep heat inside.

If you have to take a sweater off indoors because you're too warm, you are wasting money — turn the central heating down.

Hot water costs more than cold water. Not everybody knows this, so now you do if you didn't.

Change a 100W light bulb to a 60W one which costs 60 per cent as much to operate.

Use no electricity at all for one day. Of course, don't throw the switch if you have a freezer! By the end of the day you will undoubtedly have an inkling about how much entertainment eats into your budget.

Instead of watching TV, read something . . . anything. Cereal boxes or junk mail if you have to . . . or get out that sketch pad you 'haven't had time to use'.

Turn off unnecessary lights. It's all right to use electricity, but not to WASTE it.

Read your electricity meter once a week — write it down. After about three weeks you should see a pattern. Now change that pattern. Downwards.

Last one out TURN OUT THE LIGHTS.

Is anyone watching the TV?

Buy British-grown foods in season. It isn't just being economical for yourself, it really and truly is helping the country, and ultimately back to your own wallet.

Don't waste your hard-earned money by not complaining if you have purchased something which is unsatisfactory.

If you're complaining about a service or product, do it in writing, because phoning is expensive and companies are very adept at transferring you from one department to another.

Swap a service or goods with someone.

Citrus fruit pips usually germinate into lovely small plants, and turn something that was going to be thrown away into something that lasts a very long time and gives a great deal of enjoyment for no extra money.

Smoking burns money. Give it up for one day!

Remember that when you buy something you are actually making TWO choices: you are choosing — or are obligated — to buy that something and therefore you are also choosing NOT TO BUY some other thing, i.e., you must forgo another purchase of that same value.

'Needs' expand to eat all available income.

Buy less. Use less. Waste less.

Hire a video instead of going to the cinema.

Don't hire a video at all — read a book instead.

Borrow — and return on time — a book from the library. Libraries are still free so long as you don't incur fines for overdue books.

Whether you want it or not, you have paid for the public library service through your taxes, so you might as well as get some use out of it. The more you use it the lower the cost per pound of tax paid. Libraries are an opportunity to sample authors when you are uncertain whether you want to invest in a book written by them. Libraries have time-tables for trains and buses. Libraries are full of books on every craft and skill the DIY enthusiast can need. Use them.

If you don't have a babysitting group, form one. You clock up hours, not pounds.

Radio is cheaper than TV.

Do you THROW AWAY food? Make one meal a week clear-out-the-fridge. Don't buy too much in the first place. Plan ahead.

Keep a record of every single penny you spend for at least one month — you'll learn a lot.

Instead of staying in luxury — or even ordinary — hotels, have a look at bed-and-breakfasts.

Every day you should work on something that will last longer than you do. Don't worry if your artistic talent is not that of Michelangelo — time has a way of bridging the gap; the quilt you make this year may be imperfect (you do know, don't you, that a quilt SHOULD ALWAYS have an error in it?), but it will be your children's and grandchildren's heirloom to be treasured, probably simply because you made it.

We thought you would like to know . . .

If you don't already know how to do it, learn how to balance your bank statement. It does NOT tell you how much money you have. A bank statement is just that: a statement from the bank telling you what has GONE THROUGH your account AT THE BANK so far that month. If you want to know how much money you REALLY have on the date of that statement you must do a bank balance, or 'reconciliation'. Do this the minute your statement comes in.

Banks do not exist to help people. Banks exist to help banks make money — that is their business. They are not marriage guidance counsellors or crisis counsellors. If a crisis looms, the Citizens' Advice Bureau IS there to help people. Use it. It's free. It's good.

Pay bills at your bank instead of posting them, if they have Giro forms included.

Turn all your attention to getting rid of your bank overdraft. This is a lot easier said than done. Persevere.

Know what MUST be paid and what you can afford.

Make leisure time money-saving time. Take a walk and see how much food for free you can find. There are sloes, rosehips, blackberries and elderberries everywhere you look in the autumn, dandelions in the summer, sorrel in the spring. Know what you are looking at, though. There are excellent books available on wild edible plants around the world. Do not eat small Arctic buttercups — you will regret it. On the other hand, learn to recognise the Australian water tree, and South Africa is blessed with the stapelia. Be wary of fungi.

One of the prettiest packages under the Christmas tree is the one wrapped in a calendar page.

Christmas isn't just for December, it's for life. It should never come as a surprise, it comes round at exactly the same time every year — plan ahead.

Most of the best money spent on your house will probably not be visible. Learn how to spend wisely on your biggest investment — it isn't dried flowers or pretty curtains that protect the brickwork, but a coat of sealer that doesn't show.

Cut Brillo pads, nylon scourers, dusters, sponges and so on in half before using them — they go twice as far that way.

Cotton underwear makes superb cleaning cloths.

You do not have to have a battery of cleaners to keep a house clean! Many of them are quite dangerous. Washing-up liquid, vinegar and bicarbonate of soda are mild, but powerful cleaners. Choose a dry powder, such as own-brand 'floor and wall cleaner', which you can mix in varying proportions according to the cleaning job you're doing. If you read the list of ingredients, you'll find bicarbonate of soda is one of the main constituents anyway. That wonderful pine smell doesn't do a lot of cleaning. Washing-up liquid and water works on every kind of plastic known (to me, at least), and not much of either of them — just a slightly damp cloth.

No home should be without it

Vinegar is the penny pincher's friend, both as cleaner and disinfectant. You can wipe cupboards and bread bins with a vinegar-soaked cloth to help prevent mould!

The best shower-door cleaner is white vinegar. Wipe it on, leave to soak for a few minutes if the door has disappeared under a layer of white gunge, then rinse it well and polish dry. Impressive.

To absorb cooking odours, a saucer of vinegar beside the cooker does wonders. Cabbage has a way of filling the house which doesn't elicit the 'mmmmm' that bread or coffee manages.

Vinegar cleans tiles, gets rid of soapy residue on bathroom tiles.

Keep a bottle of half vinegar/half water to neutralise baby and pet puddles on carpets and furnishings instead of using expensive chemicals.

25

For a quick and easy air freshener, keep a spray bottle filled with half-and-half water and vinegar.

You can dispense with fabric softener (no pun intended). Vinegar is an excellent substitute, and many people are allergic to the materials used in softeners.

Clean vacuum flasks with a soak of half vinegar/half water, then rinse with clear water.

Descale the kettle by boiling up half-and-half vinegar and water solution, leave overnight.

Two for the price of one: mix equal quantities of white vinegar and warm water, use to wash your windows — clean windows and soft hands.

You don't actually need proprietary window cleaners at all. Vinegar and water work wonderfully, and even that can be skipped by using newspaper, water and elbow grease.

One word of caution: vinegar is acidic and therefore can damage some surfaces such as marble, stone and quarry tiles. On any surface, especially if you have used it neat, rinse well afterwards just to be sure it isn't still active.

Cut off any good fingers from rubber gloves you're discarding and use as fingershields — and you can chop the rest of the gloves into rubber bands, too.

Don't assume that just because it's a 'household hint' it is a money-saving one. Rubbing ANYTHING with a cut lemon is expensive.

Old tights or stockings can be used as nylon scourers.

When you have a spare moment, sit down and work out whether working part-time is actually worth it! Do you use that extra money to buy more expensive convenience foods, and extra clothes that you wouldn't need if you stayed at home? Would you prefer to stay at home? Why not work from home?

The very best air freshener? Fresh air! Open the window for a little while — it's free. This one saves pounds, especially in the summer. Air fresheners do not freshen air, they block your sense of smell.

Pets will usually choose a comfortable old cardboard box with a blanket or discarded sweater of yours instead of an expensive wicker basket designer pet bed. Pets are smart.

There are many, many four-letter words in our wonderful English language, but 'housewife' is not one of them.

A hot toddy doesn't have to have alcohol in it — try lemon and honey on their own. It must be good for you!

A tea mug holds approximately ten fluid ounces. A kettle holds approximately 50 fluid ounces. Boil only as much as you need to fill the mug and cover the element.

27

It is perfectly possible to cut rolls of cling film, greaseproof and foil in half.

Non-iron, permanent press fabric is a modern miracle. The Americans have unsurpassable ones which truly come through the tumble dryer without needing 'touching up' with the iron.

It costs nothing extra to wash a few cloth table napkins in a load of laundry, especially if you've chosen a non-iron fabric. Consider the price of paper napkins, and how much more civilised are cloth ones.

Cut a spongette in half and keep it on the handbasin. After every use, wipe over with the spongette. About once a week, rinse the spongette with a little vinegar and water to keep it fresh. Bath cleaners are not one of life's necessities. A little washing-up liquid added to bath water avoids high-tide marks and makes expensive cleaners unnecessary.

Food goes on cooking for several minutes after you turn off the source of heat. Therefore, turn off sources of heat a few minutes early — 365 days of several minutes' saved energy mount up.

Pine cones burn.

Dispensers are WONDERFUL for controlling amounts of washing-up liquid, shampoo, hand creams, cleansing liquids, etc., but remember: you don't have to push the plunger all the way down!!

Take a leaf out of history — particularly if you grow your own herbs such as rosemary and lavender — and strew a few in the hallway where they will freshen and welcome.

Short letters can be written on short pages. A second letter can be written on the chopped-off piece.

28

Surely, surely everybody relegates their old toothbrush to the cleaning box or shoe polishing kit . . . don't they?

Turn down your central heating by one degree Centigrade and you will save approximately 8 per cent on your annual bill. (Somehow it ought to work, therefore, that if you turn it down by 10 degrees Centigrade you're almost heating for free, but who worked out 8 per cent in the first place? Starting from where, for goodness' sake?)

It doesn't always work out cheaper to run your central heating system on a time cycle, switching on and off. If the house gets cold, then has condensation, it can be more expensive to heat it back up again and you have the condensation problem as well. CHECK your meter for a week each at least, first with the timed cycle as usual, then on constant BUT AT A LOWER TEMPERATURE. Choose the cheapest way. Every house is different, every system is different. Know your own, and use it efficiently.

Always remember: just because a washing-up bowl holds a gallon of water is no reason to put a gallon of hot water in it if half that much will do.

Use a smaller washing-up bowl, and keep the water hotter by NOT stacking all the cold dishes into the bowl.

As you become a practised penny pincher, keep your sense of humour intact. Remember that you will become somebody else's nut case, and some of your friends will have many a giggle, but it's your wallet that has to pay all the bills, not theirs. Be a happy nut case.

One of the biggest money-savers there is: take care of what you have. Maintenance works.

The money you earn is taxed, the money you save is not.

Cosset your carpets

Learn to remove stains and spots from your carpets — they are among the most expensive things in your house. Be sure that they are stain-resistant when you buy them, and then never, never, never let anything like washing-up liquid touch them! Detergents leave a sticky residue, which attracts more dirt and quite likely changes the colour of the carpet where they have been used. One roll of paper towels was a cheap price to pay for completely removing a glass of port from a white carpet. If for no other reason than that, do not eschew paper towels — just don't use them for every drop of water you spill.

Vacuuming a carpet gets the dirt out of it. This dirt will, as the carpet is walked on, cut the carpet fibres. Clean carpets make money sense.

Take off outdoor shoes when you get home — makes the shoes last longer and prevents even more dirt being deposited on your carpets.

Floors do not have to have wall-to-wall carpets. A sanded and sealed wooden floor can look very nice, and is a lot cheaper.

If you doubt the efficacy of bicarbonate of soda, just try sprinkling a bit in your shoes.

A shower takes less water than a bath, and a lick-and-promise session at the sink takes less than a shower. Here's another statistic (why do we tend to believe statistics instead of accepting what common sense tells us has been true all along?). A shower takes approximately seven gallons of water. A bath takes approximately 22 gallons of water. The compiler of these statistics obviously was not the possessor of teenagers. Parents of teenagers know that showers take 22 gallons, baths take 83 gallons.

If you are 'too busy' to do meals that require long, slow cooking (these are usually the least expensive), learn to use your timed oven or try a slow-cooker. Then you can buy cheaper cuts of meat.

Just as the only policeman that counts is the one inside us, the only penny pincher that makes a difference is the one you learn to be yourself.

You know you are winning when the children ask you what you want for your birthday, and you can honestly say that there is nothing you want. Of course you could think up things for them to buy, but you would not feel any better if they got them for you.

All the paintings on our walls have been done by us. They may not be good, but it is the only way we could afford original art.

There is nothing on television tonight that is worth watching, there was nothing last night, and there won't be anything tomorrow, so you might as well spend the evening working on the house.

Yachts cannot all be owned by millionaires, so the truth has to be that other people have different spending patterns from us, patterns that mean that they save on some things to have the money for what they really want, which is a yacht.

31

Credit cards have their uses, but handle them with care or they will eat you alive. They are marvellous if you want to buy something over the phone, like an airline ticket, but never, ever use them as a way of borrowing. I have a letter in front of me, offering me a new credit card with an 'attractive interest rate of 19.9 per cent APR.' I would hate to see an unattractive interest rate! As I write inflation is at 3.4 per cent and bank interest rate is 6 per cent. Nobody can afford to borrow at 16.5 per cent above the rate of inflation. Nothing you can buy can excuse giving that sort of money to a financial institution.

If you need to send a parcel anywhere in the world there are lots of companies that will promise a super-efficient, overnight service. And charge you for it. Very few parcels have to be delivered next day. Next month is often good enough. Ask what their slow service would cost. The Post Office is as good as any.

There is no such thing as 0 per cent interest. When you see that advertised, it simply means that the cost of the interest is in the purchase price. If you are in a position to pay cash, then ask for this money back. The salesman will give you a lot of guff, but ask to speak to the manager, and he may well cut the price to you for cash.

Computers are used by companies to save money. If you have a computer at home, use it the same way. Use the spreadsheet to help with budgeting. Keep your bank balance on it. Store good recipes in memory, and use it so that you do not forget important dates. Draft out a letter, and only when you are satisfied with it, print it. That saves paper.

It is a curious thing that we buy magazines concerned with fashion and with cars, full of articles and advertisements for things we cannot afford and would not enjoy if we had, illustrated in the lives of the most useless members of society. Save the price of the magazines and the corrosion of temptation by leaving the magazines on the shelf.

Recycling the recycled

To help keep Christmas ornaments from getting broken, wrap them in newspaper and store in strong cardboard boxes. Small delicate ones can spend the year in egg boxes.

Children don't need expensive art and craft materials — they're right in front of you, with newspapers that they can draw on, tear, cut, glue, colour, find words or use to make up their own puzzles.

You won't worry so much about children making a mess of things if you underlay THEM with acres of newspaper — under the high chair, under tables while they're playing at them, near the sink while they 'help' wash up.

A large sheet of newspaper and a ridiculously large bow make a most cheeerful wrap for large gifts.

Newspapers are good drawer, shelf and cupboard liners.

Shredded newspaper makes superb cat litter. Experiment to find the most absorbent.

One of the cheaper games in life is 'Are you there, Moriarty?' which only requires a rolled-up newspaper and a blindfold. If you can't get a few laughs out of that, you are taking yourself much too seriously.

Newspaper is cheap as packing material! Use it to protect your china and glass in a house move.

Save a small fortune by 1) giving up smoking, and 2) not using the expensive nicotine gums but chewing a little bit of beeswax instead.

Rule Number One: KNOW what you can afford. Spelt K-N-O-W, not H-O-P-E.

In Victorian times it was remarked that the rich man buying ten tons of coal paid less per ton than the poor man buying a half-hundredweight. This still applies, and buying in bulk can save you money, provided the product will be used, and you have the storage room.

A tip that gives a 100 per cent saving: don't buy it. Then a few days later note with pleasure how often you are glad you didn't.

Shaving up bitty pieces of soap to make a new bar will never make you rich, but it will make you a little less poor. If you make enough little savings, one day you may not be poor.

In every month there is one totally unexpected bill for £50. Add into your budget a line labelled 'unexpected £50 bill'.

Do, please, pay the local tradesmen when their money is due, for being self-employed is hard work today. We may take a rather more detached view of big national companies, however. The utility companies have various levels of agitation, from the original invoice to the Final Demand. Find out how many steps they go through, and organise to pay at the moment before cut-off. This keeps the money in your account and not theirs, and they have lots more than you do.

If there is a fax machine already installed, it makes sense to use it. Faxes cut out all the useless chit-chat about your health and the weather, and writing it down makes you organise your thoughts. Then the fax can be sent at the cheapest rate!

Every time you go to a burger-bar think about the huge and luscious steak you could have bought with the same money.

'Let the little one's clothes be always spotlessly clean, neat and well-fitting, but remember that the more simply a child is dressed the better she will look, whilst an over-dressed child will invariably lay her parents open to the charge of vulgarity.'
The Woman's Book, 1911.

As a rule, in a husband-and-wife business, the man runs around having ideas, seeing customers and generally waving his arms about, while the woman looks after the money. Both roles are vital to the success of the company, but women make the best penny-pinchers.

2
SHOPPING

Write out a list of what you need to buy before you go shopping. Clutch the list in your fat little paw. Do not leave it on the sideboard or desk. Take it with you, refer to it often, and resist the temptation to buy something you see that isn't on your list.

Open patterns in china are so often closed. Learn to love mix and match.

Buy a large tin of instant coffee instead of several jars over several weeks. The difference in price is substantial.

Buy an own-brand large tin of instant coffee instead of a brand-name one.

Silicone baking paper lasts longer than greaseproof.

Buy a flexible plastic spatula which is just the right size and shape for scooping every last bit of food out of every container known to mankind.

Very small spiral notebook, 'name' office-supply shop: £1.89. Large spiral notebook, from small newsagent: 42p.

Jumble sales and car boot sales are treasure troves of old tools. Buy only from stallholders who do not look as though they have used one of them to gain possession from a former owner.

Never go grocery shopping when you're hungry — eat something. Anything. Otherwise everything looks inviting and you buy more than you intended.

Shops manipulate you: First they study you, then they take full advantage of that study to encourage you to buy more goods than you intend. They know where you look when you walk into a store. They know what colours attract you. They stack their shelves so that you have to bend down to pick up staple items and your eyes are looking at expensive ones . . . so . . . WHY DON'T YOU STUDY THEM AND USE THAT STUDY TO YOUR ADVANTAGE.

Use three coinpurses . . . not separate ones, but one inside another; while you're getting to your money you may decide you don't want to spend it after all.

Know how much things cost. How can you tell something is a bargain otherwise?

Look for bargains, and be sure it IS a bargain — there may be 75p off this week, but is it still 45p more than it would cost elsewhere?

Use a big-business principle when buying things — JIT: Just In Time. Don't tie up money in goods not yet needed, especially if you have an overdraft.

Buy own-brand goods if you are shopping in a superstore. Very often, there is no difference at all between those goods and brand-name ones except for the label.

Shop at more than one place if you possibly can. They all work on 'swings and roundabouts' and if one thing is cheap, another has to be expensive. Choose the cheap at each shop.

Double (or more) saving: say no to children whining for sweets — save money on sweets and even more money on dentistry.

Buy a nine-pack loo roll instead of brand-name ones.

Buy a 28lb (12 kilo) bag of potatoes. This is a huge saving, and even if you throw away the last pound or so of spuds, it will STILL be a large saving. If you enjoy playing with a calculator, compare the price of crisps per ounce with the price of a 28lb (12 kilo) bag of potatoes per ounce.

Buy a 500g box of bicarbonate of soda from the chemists' instead of small boxes from the grocers'.

Do a whole shopping session without buying a single brand-name item.

Buy a pair of shoes from a discount outlet.

If you're window-shopping, don't be tempted to go inside at all to 'have a closer look'.

To save time and money in your most-frequented shop, MAP IT, and then make your shopping list in that order. Organised. No backtracking. And when the shelves are rearranged so that you have to look for everything in a new aisle, draw your map again.

Don't buy things on credit cards unless you can afford to pay it all off when the statement arrives. Don't think that somehow the money will be there — it probably won't.

COMPARE PRICES between shops. (You're supposed to choose the lower one, by the way.)

Don't just use the same superstore or chemist all the time; even if you work full time you might be able to alternate shops and pick up the bargains at each. It doesn't take long to learn which items are a little bit overpriced at which shop.

Compare the cost of chicken pieces per pound and a whole chicken per pound. Are you REALLY that busy?

Buy a £3.99 bottle of wine instead of a £4.99 one.

Look for book sales at your local library. Their prices are usually good, and not all the books are 1967 road atlases.

If you do have a card for a wholesale outlet you need to know retail prices — sometimes you can end up paying more than you would on the high street.

Second-hand bookshops are a hobby in themselves, because the search for a book — or a collection of books — can be as much enjoyment as reading the books themselves.

All the great literature of the English language can be found in second-hand bookshops, as well as great trash. When poking through the dusty shelves one does wonder about the people who bought the books when new, but there are old authors, new to me, who have given great pleasure. The bindings on old books are often much better than on new ones, and they are affordable.

As a general rule, you don't have to rush out and buy things the minute you decide you need them.

Markets are ancient. They survive because they work. Millions have found bargains there. Join them.

Save for purchases rather than using expensive credit.

While you're saving, you may well decide you don't need or want the item anyway.

LISTEN to friends and family all during the year, and you'll find you are rarely at a loss as to what someone wants for Christmas.

Determine when your favourite shops have special offers — often it's first thing Monday morning, sometimes last thing on Saturday afternoon. Try to shop then, and pounds can be saved. Greengrocers are treasure troves of very ripe bananas for something like 5p or 10p per pound — banana bread takes approximately 25-30 seconds to whizz up in a food processor. Living better for less!!

Buy only what you need, but buy enough so that it will last you until the next shopping trip — you aren't saving money if you're always popping into the shops to top up supplies.

You really do have to compare prices when you're shopping — sometimes it is cheaper to buy two smaller-sized tins of a product rather than one larger tin. If your mental maths aren't up to it, take a calculator!

Check the weight on tins and jars — two that are similar in price may vary enormously in size although they LOOK the same.

Check NET contents weight — two different brands of beans which are exactly the same size may differ greatly in the amount of beans inside. If you like lots of juice, fine, but be aware that you're getting more juice in that brand. And it's no good complaining afterwards, it does give the weight on the label!

Learn to say — to yourself at least — 'I can't afford that item.'

As a general rule, the large supermarkets are cheaper than the corner shop, but not if you let yourself yield to every temptation the supermarkets dangle before you — and they are experts at that!

Take advantage of special offers on products that you know you will use! This is an area where it's easier said than done if you are on a very tight budget, but if you can squeeze pennies in other places, you can save a lot on specials.

DON'T stock up with huge quantities of anything expensive unless you know you WILL use it all before it swells up, turns black and dies.

Supermarkets are almost always more expensive than greengrocers — and they never seem to have that wonderful corner where bananas smell so good as they reach banana-bread perfection and purse-friendly price.

Unless you are AT Wimbledon, don't buy strawberries during Wimbledon.

Advertisers would have you believe that you deserve only the very best — and the most expensive. Do you think that advertisers are working for you . . . or for the product?

Read the label: 'best before' is not 'USE before'. Don't lazily depend on 'the government' to make decisions that you should make for yourself.

Loose vegetables are cheaper than plastic-wrapped ones. You do already know that, don't you? If this piece of information has come as a surprise to you, you have got a real shopping problem.

It is easier to shop without children, so try to do it during school hours.

Local newspapers have pages of small ads for things people are selling — check these before you rush out and buy something new. Second-hand things are sometimes real treasures.

Write out your shopping list. At the bottom of it, draw a line right across the page. As you shop, write down anything that you realise you need and buy in addition to the things on the list. With practice, you will be able to make better lists.

Reward yourself on your list! Write down the things that you saw which you would have bought before you started taking care of your money — write down how much they cost. Do not be tempted to blow it somewhere else just because you 'saved' a few pounds.

Keep a list of 'staples' — things that you buy every time you go into the grocery shop or that you always keep in stock. You may treat these as 'impulse' buys if you see them on special even if they aren't on your shopping list for that week.

If you are shopping around for furniture, have a look at an auction — they're always around, but you MUST know your prices. It's all too easy to become determined you are going to have an item and start bidding against some old crone in the corner, and you end up paying a lot more than you would have done in the high street.

Coupons are almost invariably money off products you oughtn't to be buying if you're penny-pinching.

Don't spend a pound's worth of petrol driving across the country to save twenty-five pence.

When you have spent too much on groceries, look through what you've bought. Chances are that there are more 'convenience foods' than there are 'real' foods and staple items such as flour, margarine and milk.

The Post Office puts up the price of stamps about once a year, and then all the stamps we have in the house are a penny or two too little, so we have to buy more stamps to make up the difference. Buy your stamps with First or Second, but not the price, on them. The Post Office will continue to honour these stamps bought at the old price after the price increase has gone through.

Supermarkets seem to have more items on special price on Mondays than any other day, so that makes Monday a good day to visit them. A lot of the items on special will just be the usual overpacked, over-prepared foods, so we can ignore those and look for the real foods. Often the bargains will be marked with a coloured sticker that makes them easy to pick out.

You do know about visual brighteners in washing powders, don't you? Don't pay a premium for powders that make your clothes glow in the dark!

Shop first with your pencil and paper, then the phone and Yellow Pages, and finally with your wallet.

Whether you're leafing through a glossy magazine or strolling through any shop, be on the watch for those words that make you not only want something, but try to make you think that YOU OWE IT TO YOURSELF to buy it. Not for nothing are they wordsmiths of the advertising world: 'appropriate, crafted, distinctive, DESERVE, LUXURIOUS, graceful, fragrant, charming'. Beware the realms of wish and want.

3
DIY

Glue a piece of felt on the bottom of a ceramic tile for a heat-resistant mat.

Save as much wood scrap as you have room to store — you always need odd bits and pieces.

Mix sawdust with wood glue to make tight dowel joins or repairs to furniture.

You can make up your own 'plastic wood' as you need it by mixing fine sawdust with some synthetic glue. Add dry pigment to match the colour of the piece you're repairing.

If you don't make enough sawdust and shavings in your own workshop for all the uses they have, visit any timber mill or woodworking business. They will be grateful for your takeaway service.

You can use plastic sheeting as double glazing over windows. You may even be able to find a converter or stockholder who is willing to sell you seconds.

Repair an item instead of replacing it.

Make your own pastes, glues and play doughs with salt, flour and water.

Paint a wall instead of wallpapering it — the difference in cost is substantial, and you can see what is going on with the wall. Wallpaper may hide a multitude of sins, but it also hides problems that you ought to be monitoring.

Toys don't have to be brightly-coloured plastic. You can make lovely toys in wood or fabric and they'll probably last longer as well.

You are clever. Make up your own board games. They might even be so much better than the ones on the market that you have a whole new career before you.

If you like making little miniature flower decorations, take another look at bottle-tops, which can be quite ornate.

You can make artificial flowers from florists' wire and nylon tights; while I personally wouldn't stick them in a vase, they can be fun as a gift bow, or you could tuck some into a fun hat. Children enjoy making them.

Chopped up tights and stockings make washable stuffing for toys and last FOREVER.

To save hundreds, if not thousands, of pounds, you can 'do' your own wedding. You may go grey in the process, but it is enjoyable, rewarding and memorable.

If you can make a Christmas cake, you can make a wedding cake.

Decorate your own Easter eggs by using onion skins and flowers and vegetables from the garden and hedgerow for colour — wet the eggs (white ones work best), press a few flower petals on, wrap with outer brown onion skins for a 'gilded' look, secure with strips of cloth, string, even rubber bands. Omit the onion skins for other colours. Add vegetables from the garden, fruits from the freezer, to boiling water, drop in the egg mummies and hardboil. Spinach, beetroot, blackberries, damsons, gorse blossom all give beautiful colours. No two are ever alike.

Make tiny baubles for the Christmas tree from a gaudy, large, shiny necklace (jumble sales and charity shops will have them). String a large bead with two or three small ones, hang with paper clip.

If you're frightfully artistic, try vegetable peels in a Christmas wreath or flower arrangement.

Recognise your limits — in money, time and talents. If you don't know enough about electricity to change a plug, you'd be pretty daft to set about wiring a house.

Marble mantels can often lurk under several coats of paint. Marble mantels can easily be ruined. Carefully scrape off paint — use no chemicals! Get the last bits out with fine wire wool. Polish with beeswax-turpentine furniture polish. Do not ever be tempted to clean with anything acidic (and that, of course, includes lemon juice and vinegar).

At least once a year go all round the outside of the house with a ladder, checking the gutters for blockages and damage.

You could save many hundreds of pounds if you learn how to do your own car maintenance, or plumbing, or electricals. Local colleges have wonderful courses available. Look them up in your local paper.

If you can ice a Christmas cake, you can make a plaster repair . . . eventually.

Decide whether a repair has to be a professional one immediately or whether it's something that could be a DIY hold-it-together-for-a-while one. Possibly a plaster will suffice instead of having to have stitches — the same is true about many a job where the repairman called in will suck in his breath sharply and suggest your house will fall down before sunset unless you sign up right now for him to mend the downpipe.

Old wooden pallets are excellent building materials. John built an entire stable from second-hand pallets, including making the 'tiled' roof, hanging each tile by reclaimed nails.

Sometimes building materials can be had for free. If you see a tumbledown shed that you could turn into a good fence or gate, the shed owner may be grateful to you for taking it away (ASK FIRST). You'll have to use some elbow grease, but it won't cost a lot of money. Our brother and his wife collected all the bricks to build a house from old chimney stacks and decrepit buildings lurking around the countryside, hauled them home and hand-cleaned every one of them, but that's a bargain price for a house.

When doing a repair job using cement, it is worth taking the time to make a calculation of how much cement you need for the work. There is nothing worse than nearly to complete the patch and then run out, or to have half of the mix left over, which is a waste. One is tempted to make garden gnomes of this residue, and that is always a mistake.

Paint

If you have odds and ends of paint lurking in a cupboard (and most of us do) you can mix the lot as long as they're of the same sort — i.e. emulsion or oil — and have your own designer colours. Just don't run out halfway round the room!

Lacking the courage to store tins of paint upside down, we always shake them before storing to make sure that there is a layer of paint over the lid 'seam' to keep air out.

Professional painters swear by really good expensive paintbrushes, but if you're an amateur, you might well be better off pennywise just to buy new inexpensive brushes for each job. The cost of white spirit needed to clean a brush thoroughly could well be more than a whole new brush!

Don't let your paintbrush go gungy while you're having a coffee break. Slip a plastic bag over its head, and wrap it tightly to keep out the air. You can also just dunk it in a tin of water.

Use small tins for paint instead of dipping your brush into the big tin. You will waste less paint on the small tin than you will by letting the big tin dry out or get dirty. This does assume that you don't spill the lot decanting it into the small tin!

No household is complete without a few paintbrushes that have gone hard from dried paint, or have been left in turpentine so long that the brush is surrounded with a tacky jelly. Unless the brush is a really expensive one, it is best to use these old brushes as fire lighters. Cheap brushes are now so cheap that the cost of cleaning materials does not make them worth recovering. Better yet, clean emulsion paints out of paintbrushes right after use with soap and water, and oil paints with white spirit. Then set on newspaper to dry, but not resting on the bristles.

When painting a room, especially if the colour of the paint will be used only in that room, buy no more, or even less, paint than you think you will need. You can always go back to buy more, perhaps a quarter tin to finish the job. Buying too much paint leads to those half tins of solidified paint that clutter all our paint cupboards.

The two important factors in the protection given by paint are, first, its adherence to the material being painted, and that means good preparation of the material is essential, and second, the thickness of the coat that goes on.

Don't be fooled into thinking that your eight-foot square room will look spacious if you paint it in a cool colour. The only way you can make an eight-foot square room spacious is by moving the walls. You can help the illusion of space with a bit of blue paint, but you still have an eight-foot square room, so don't try to recreate the Sistine chapel in it.

Try to live with your house instead of constantly fiddling around with it — you can spend several fortunes redecorating to keep up with the latest fashion. This year's ravishing peach is next year's out-of-date yucky orange. If you change your décor often, you're looking at too many glossy magazines.

You don't have to buy everything you see in a glossy magazine — as you thumb through the scrumptious decorating/house magazines, look at everything with a new eye: what can you make? Which things that you admire do you already have, or have something similar?

Even a kitchen can be transformed without spending a fortune: if your cupboards are still good, why not just change the doors? There are specialist firms that will do this for you, but if you're at all handy with wood, you can do it for a fraction of the cost. It's much easier these days to find the professional fittings than it was twenty years ago when we made our own from scratch.

If you do make your own kitchen furniture, remember that you can always paint wooden cupboards a different colour if you want to change later.

Wooden boxes and flush doors still stack up to make temporary furniture.

Make your own efficient, long-lasting and portable bookcase: all you need are bricks and boards. The method is simple: stack 'em.

You can make your own rugs, whether with a kit you buy or from scraps. One of the most elegant rugs I have ever seen was a tapestry one, in a stately home. On the floor, not on the wall. If you have the patience you might try doing one, but quicker is a rag rug, and this doesn't have to look scrappy, either; you can make very pretty and practical ones with narrow strips of woollen fabric.

Repair/replace broken air bricks. For some strange reason a hole in an air brick will attract a small bird who, having got in, will be quite unable to get out without the assistance of human beings, hammers, saws, etc.

Used roofing tiles can be half the price of new tiles. Some care is required, because old tiles were made by the many small manufacturers of those days, and they all manufactured to their own design and size, even when making the same type of tile. Tiles from different manufacturers will not necessarily fit neatly together. The only reliable way of getting matching tiles is to get them all from the same demolition. Ask their origin if buying them from an architectural recovery yard.

To convert kW to Btu/h, multiply by 3412. This is useful if your boiler is rated in kW and you have done your heating calculations in Btus.

Keeping warm for next to nothing

If you are extending your central heating system, think about whether it needs to be in every room. For instance, if you have an attic guest bedroom, it is probably cheaper to use an electric fire in that room than to run the central heating up there.

Temperature control valves on each radiator are real money-savers, if you turn down the heat in rooms where it is not needed. For instance, if you are not going to use the dining-room today, turn the control valve right down.

Do not be afraid to turn off the heat from a radiator, even in really cold weather. Some heat will still reach the room from the central heating pipes, keeping it above freezing.

Hot water pipes often run through parts of the house that do not need to be heated, or where heat can be detrimental, such as through larders. DIY stores can supply specially-made insulation for any size of pipe, so that heat is not lost to the wrong areas, and more heat is delivered where it it needed.

Central heating systems do not get scaled up because they use the same water that is in the system over and over again. Do not drain the central heating system, unless you have to.

Solid-fuel boilers may or may not be cheap to run, but they do produce a lot of ash that has to be cleaned up.

The old-fashioned iron radiator is extremely efficient at warming a room. Even if you are installing a new, efficient boiler, why not keep the old radiators?

If a radiator is fitted under a window, make sure the curtains are short and do not lead all the heat up the inside next to the glass, but allow the heat out into the room.

Edge the thermostat down slowly. If you reduce it drastically, the rest of the family tends to notice.

I have never seen anyone who was really satisfied with central heating from off-peak electricity, except the people on TV who advertise the system. On the other hand, it is cheap to install.

If air gets into the radiators it can cause an air block, effectively cutting the system. The air can be bled out from the little valve at the top of the each radiator, but this should only be necessary if the system has been newly installed or drained down. If air is still getting in, then there is a leak of air somewhere in the system, and this needs to be found and corrected.

Double glazing as installed by your over-friendly double glazing company is rarely a good investment if looked at simply in terms of cost against lower heating bills. Double glazing will, however, cut out draughts and also sound-proof your house, and these alone can make it well worth while.

Double glazing in a scullery or larder is hard to justify. Get some clear plastic sheeting and put it up with drawing pins. It is not pretty, but it will give you most of the benefits of double glazing.

Condensation is caused by warm, wet air hitting cold surfaces. Condensation makes rooms feel uncomfortable, it causes mould, and the wet will rot woodwork. I have successfully treated this by lining the walls of a bedroom with ⅛ inch (3mm) sheet expanded polystyrene, and then wallpapering over it.

A hot water tank needs to be lagged, otherwise that large copper surface will radiate your heat and your money. Even if you have a jacket on it, why not use old blankets, towels, and anything else you can find that will act as insulation, and wrap up the tank well?

If you are permitted to use wood-burning stoves in your area, burn old newspapers rather than throw them away. They burn well, and produce a lot of heat quickly. Don't forget to save the ash for the garden.

Agas, Rayburns and other kitchen ranges are not especially efficient in terms of heat output and cooking economy, but they are nice. Try to stop your family opening the oven door to warm their backsides or even sit in it. It is a dreadful waste of heat.

A front door and a back door lobby make a lot of difference to the heat loss of a house. If you can, close in the front and back porches, or build on, and stop that cold air sweeping in.

When you close in the front or back porch, it is usually sensible to glass it in. When it catches the sun it will act as a mini-greenhouse and that heat will transfer to the house when the inner door is opened. Also, when you answer the front door, your caller is still on the outside and you can have a good look at him or her through the glass before deciding whether to open the door.

Twenty per cent of the heat lost from a house will be through the roof. Every roof space should be insulated with at least four inches (100 mm) of glass fibre, and six inches (150 mm) is better. The cost of the glass fibre will be repaid in heat saved.

When insulating the loft space, run the insulation over and around water tanks, never underneath. A little heat will come up through the ceiling of the room below, and stop the tank from freezing. If a pipe has frozen in the attic, warm the pipe gently with a butane blow-torch or with an electric heater. Be prepared to turn off the house water supply in a hurry, because the frozen water may well have burst a pipe.

If you are using a butane blow-torch to thaw out a frozen pipe, heat it gently. It is easy to boil the water in a section of the pipe, and the steam will not melt the ice until it has burst the pipe.

High winds strip heat away from a building. If you live in a windy spot, try planting trees and bushes to cut down the wind speed. The best are evergreens planted on the side towards the prevailing wind.

A bird nesting in the roof means that there is a hole somewhere for it to get in. In winter, a howling gale will be blowing through the hole. Find out where the birds are getting in, turf the little blighters out and block up the hole.

Underlay under the carpet not only protects the carpet and makes it more comfortable to walk on, but also acts as an insulator. Here is yet another place you can use old newspapers. Put them down under the underlay, and they'll help avoid those grey lines that appear where the floorboards don't quite meet.

Should you have to replace a window, take the opportunity to make it double layered. Have one set of windows opening out, and the inner set opening in, and there is double glazing, as good as or better than anything from a double glazing company.

There is a sort of ceremony, a Rite of Spring, in America every year, when the detachable glass panes over the windows are taken down and the fly screens go up. It is an easy task to make a frame filled in with glass, and then hang it over the window during cold weather.

Little sticky strips around the windows are cheap and effective at cutting draughts.

Every house should have an effective damp course. If your house does not, you can hire the equipment from your local hire shop and buy the chemicals to put one in. If you decide to get a contractor to do the job, get quotations and ask around for satisfied users. It is a field that has more than its fair share of cowboys.

Over time it is easy for earth and debris from flowerbeds to build up outside the house, lifting the soil level above the damp course. Walk round the house and look to see that this has not happened, and that all the air bricks are clear.

Plumbing

Before calling a plumber, check to see if it is a fitting that can be tightened with a spanner. A Footprint pipewrench is a most useful tool for tightening nuts on pipes.

Don't let taps drip. Mend them. Fast.

Water leaks from pipe joints rarely fix themselves.

If the leak is from a soldered joint it will be necessary to drain down the whole system. Even a tiny amount of water near the joint will stop the solder flowing.

Save spare swear words and washers so that they are to hand for the next plumbing task.

Taps often drip from around the stem when they are turned on. To stop this, take off the handle. On cross top taps, the handle is held on by a grub screw, while the retaining screw of a moulded handle will be found under the plate on top that shows hot or cold. Ease this plate off with a screwdriver. Most taps will then have a chrome shield around the stem that has to be removed. This shield is screwed on, and it will take a plumbers' spanner to get it off. To protect the chrome, try to pad the jaws with thin material. Remove the shield. A nut, through which the stem passes, can now be seen. Turn on the tap and very gently tighten down this nut until the leak stops. It will only be a fraction of a turn. Reassemble the tap.

If a tap drips from the outlet when fully turned off, the washer needs replacing. First, turn off the water supply to that tap at a stop cock (it may be under the sink), and then turn on the tap to drain any water in the pipe. Take off the tap handle and the tap shield (see above). The body of the tap is faced to take a spanner, and so unscrew the body and the stem and take off. At the bottom end of the stem there is a washer held in place by a nut. Take off the nut and its washer, replace the washer with a new one and reassemble the tap. Turn on the water supply.

When doing any work with water pipes, first check to see if the old piping is Imperial or metric. You may need an adapter to join the two different systems and these are easy to find in a plumbers' shop. Imperial and metric fittings nearly fit each other but not quite.

When doing any work on a water system, first turn off the tap that you think controls the water to the section you are working on, and then turn on the tap or valve in the system to drain all the water out. If you have not in fact isolated the system, the second tap will continue to run. This is so much better than undoing a joint and then finding the water is still under pressure.

If a tap or plumbing joint or sink outflow has a slight drip, try gently tightening the joint first, before investing in a major replacement of the whole thing.

For the plumbingly challenged, formerly known as the clumsy, try replacing the whole fitting with a plastic Acorn fitting that can be put on without any tools. Turn off the water and drain the system first or prepare to mop.

The water level in a lavatory cistern, or any other water tank, can be adjusted by bending the arm that has the floating ball on it (with extreme caution — do not bend too far). Do not try to get too much water in the lavatory cistern, because this wastes water, and also because water will slowly leak out around the blanking plate on the side opposite to the handle. One of our neighbours over-adjusted his cistern and then went on holiday. He came back to find that the slow leak had soaked the ceiling of the hall and the plaster had collapsed onto the floor.

We all have big ideas about the changes we want to make when moving to a new house. Resist the temptation to start work straight away. Live in the house for six months, and you may find that the way things are is pretty sensible, and the planned work is not needed at all. Some people who bought a house from us ripped out the adequate if ordinary kitchen, and replaced it with a wonderfully smart and expensive one. The new owner then stood in her transformed room and told us that it had cost more than she had intended, and she did not like it very much. With a little patience, the urge to spend may pass.

A conservatory attached to the house will warm up even on cold winter days. When it gets warm, open the door into your house and get free solar heat.

Use old squares of carpet in lobbies and at outside doors as door mats. When they get really dirty, throw them away.

Few of us are gifted craftsmen, so we need to make up for our deficiencies. One way is to buy the best materials possible, and buy for our own use the best tools (except in the case of paintbrushes). Good tools and good materials are nearly always easier to handle and will give a better result. A good craftsman can take poor materials and, with simple tools, create wondrous things. Most of us are not that good.

Building regulations are there to protect us from ourselves, and to protect our neighbours from us. If there is the possibility that the work you are about to undertake could fall within the rules of the building regulations, then phone your local council and ask. The cost of flouting building regulations can be very high.

Man is defined as the tool-using animal. People who say they are no good with machinery, or they just cannot understand computers, are denying a large part of their humanity. The most likely reason is that they are lazy.

An open fire is a picturesque and welcoming feature in any room, but it is about as inefficient a way of heating as can be devised. Most of the heat goes up the chimney. A better room heater is a free-standing stove with a glass front. The whole body of the stove takes heat from the fire and radiates it back into the room.

Carpet basics

If there are small children in your house, consider having a carpet in the kitchen. Carpets are now specially made for kitchens and they are easy to keep clean. Even if they are relatively expensive, you will make a saving on dishes and glasses, since these then have a good chance of surviving being dropped. It is a fact of growth that children will drop plates and glasses, and they are a goner on tiled floors and other hard surfaces.

If a fitted carpet is worn or badly stained in one place, it will be cheaper to buy a good rug to cover the spot than to replace the whole carpet.

Stair carpets become worn on the front edge of the tread, while the vertical piece, the riser, remains almost unworn. Even the wear by taking up the carpet and shifting it down half a step, so that the riser is now on the step, and the old steps are now risers. It is necessary to cut off the bottom half-step and tack this on to the top riser, but this small loss of neatness is justfied by the gain in the life of the carpet.

If there is fresh blood on your carpet — and we will not ask why there is fresh blood on your carpet — it can be removed. Blot up with a cloth and clean, cold, water. If stains remain, try a few drops of hydrogen peroxide left on for a few minutes, and then use a cloth and cold water again.

Demolition sites are a grand source of wood, doors, windows and tiles for the penny pincher. Ask for the site foreman and strike a deal with him for what you want. Nearly everything on a site will be thrown away, so you are helping to recycle resources by using these materials.

'If it ain't broke, don't fix it' is a good maxim, and it is cheap.

If the urge to modernise your bathtub, sinks and lavatories sweeps over you, resist. Leave the fittings where they are for the next twenty years, and at the end of that time, they will have transformed themselves into highly desirable features. An example would be lavatories with high cistern and chain pulls. This, of course, does not apply to anything coloured avocado and made of plastic.

Hot grease from cooking poured down the sink cools as it passes through the house drains and out towards the sewer. As it cools, it solidifies, and this lump can become entangled with any small obstruction in the drain. The best way to avoid having to call out someone to clear the drain is to put all waste cooking fat in an empty container, such as an empty milk carton or tin, and dispose of that in the dustbin.

If your drains get blocked fairly frequently, then look for the cause. It is likely to be tree roots growing into the pipe, or the pipe may be broken. It will be cheaper to remove the cause than to treat the symptom.

If there are long drain runs on your property, then drain rods are a good investment. The cost of the rods will often be less than a single call-out of a commercial drain-clearing company. Clearing drains is not pleasant, but you made the mess.

When replacing a window, get the glass cut ⅛ inch (3 mm) smaller than the size of the frame. Clean out all the old putty, then put a small bead of new putty against the back of the window frame to seat the new glass. Secure the glass by driving small nails into the frame to hold the glass, and then putty the window in. A kitchen knife will be a useful smoothing tool. Leave for a week before painting, but it may be necessary to protect the putty from blue tits in winter. They love the linseed oil in the putty.

Here's how to straighten a nail. The want of a nail can hold up a job, so it is worth it to save all nails pulled out of old work. Put the bent nail on a hard surface and hold down the point with the left hand, while tapping on the nail with a light hammer. A very badly bent nail can sometimes be straightened by putting it horizontally in a vice and squeezing the nail until it is nearly straight, and then finish as above.

Save screws taken from old work, unless the threads have begun to strip. If the shoulders of the slot are at all damaged, it is better to throw the screw away.

Before throwing a piece of equipment away, try to disassemble to get at least the nuts and bolts off, and then thread them together again, before storing in a box. A wide selection of nuts, bolts and washers will always come in useful.

Reclaimed timber is often a better buy than new timber. The place to find a supplier of reclaimed timber is in the Yellow Pages, and if you go to the yard you will find timber that has been salvaged from offices, churches and houses. There will be everything from floorboards to rafters. Pick up a piece and note the weight. Most of it is much heavier, i.e. denser, than new timber. It is dirty and it probably has nails in it, but, size for size, it can be half the price of new, and a lot stronger. If you have any suspicion that there may be rot in the wood, then treat it with a proprietary wood preserver.

If it becomes necessary to lift a floorboard to get at a pipe joint, or at an electrical junction box, do not nail the boards back, but screw them down. Then, if the same place gives trouble again, it will be easy to get at it.

If you live in a town and want to keep livestock, the only thing is bees. They do better than in the country, because towns are a little warmer, and the long season of flowers from cultivated gardens gives them food. Half of England is convinced that they will die if they are stung by a bee. This is nonsense, or our ancestors would have all been killed off when bees were kept as the only source of sweetness. On the other hand, it is not a bad story to put about, for it may keep vandals out of your garden.

Thick curtains are an added layer of insulation and they save heat. Thick curtains will also protect alcohol-crazed eyeballs from direct sunlight.

Furniture for less than a fortune

Modern furniture, with its straight lines, is easy to make. The best designs can be seen in your chosen store, and then measure it up on the spot and write it down. Then go home and make it.

Decent wood furniture is made strong by well-made joints — mortise and tenon, dovetail, by the use of dowels, and so on. Furniture tends to fall apart at the joints because the glue has gone after many years, and a good repair will involve taking the joint completely apart, cleaning out the old glue, and re-glueing with a modern furniture glue. There is no point trying to force glue into an assembled joint; it will not work.

Re-upholstering furniture can save you an awful lot of money, but you really ought to take a class first. We've done quite a bit of simple re-doing, but finally had a go at a chair, without the benefit of a class. Being of practical natures, we took photographs as we disembowelled it, so that we could see exactly how it went back together. Finally, as it stood in the middle of the attic room, a bare wooden frame of little resemblance to the fat comfortable seat of the week before, the film was eagerly awaited. Alas, it had never 'caught' on the spool of the old second-hand camera, and we spent a small fortune on the phone to our friend who had done a class.

Stripping off old paint, however, is quite another matter. We found the cheapest and best method of all was simply to use a scraping tool, sandpaper and elbow grease. No chemicals. No napalm.

One of the cheapest and best tools for dealing with furniture from which you've removed the paint is a sandpaper sponge. Cheap and wonderful.

Buying old furniture, and then cleaning, stripping repairing and polishing it will give you a houseful of furniture that will be a credit to you, while spending twice the sum on new furniture will still give you something pretty ordinary.

If a repair to a piece of furniture requires, say, a piece of oak, it is often cheaper to go to a sale and buy an old and ugly oak wardrobe and knock it apart to get the piece you want, than to buy the oak from a timber merchant.

If a piece of furniture or a door has to be stripped, it is cheaper to go to a commercial stripper, who has a vat of stripper into which the whole piece can be dipped, than to do it yourself.

White rings on a polished surface can be removed by rubbing it out using very fine steel wool (grade 000) and linseed oil. Wipe clean, and polish.

Another method of removing white rings from polished wood: Mix together four parts olive oil to one part paraffin wax, and heat gently until the wax has melted. When cool, rub this on marks, leave half an hour and wipe off. Repeat if necessary. Only just short of a miracle. A jar of this is always in the cleaning box.

Make your own furniture polish by mixing equal parts vinegar, pure turpentine and boiling water. Let it cool before using.

The best furniture cleaner ever, and worth trying before you start refinishing a piece, is: two parts vinegar, three parts pure turpentine, three parts boiled linseed oil. Add a small amount of elbow grease, a couple of old rags, and you may need do nothing else to that grotty old chest of drawers or cupboard.

Did you know that woodworm only enters furniture at unpolished surfaces? Therefore, once a year it would be wise to polish the whole piece with beeswax-turpentine polish.

Beeswax polish: three times as much PURE TURPENTINE as beeswax (ie, 100g beeswax, 300ml turpentine). Do not use turps or white spirit! Gently melt the beeswax — remember it is flammable — and stir in the turpentine. Pour into a jar or plastic screwtop container, leave to cool before putting on the lid. Adjust proportions to suit — if you want a thinner polish, add more turpentine, or for a harder wax polish use less turpentine. Incredibly wonderful for furniture, leather, metals. Don't forget there's one other ingredient that must be added: elbow grease. On the other hand, you really only need apply this polish about once a year — just dust off in the interim period.

Fill in scratches on furniture with a piece of beeswax. If the furniture is dark, you can rub it first with a piece of nut such as walnut, pecan or Brazil — all of which are oily ones — to restore a great deal of the colour.

Repointing brickwork is tedious, but well within the ability range of any householder. It takes time, and is therefore expensive, if done by a contractor. Repointing is needed when the cement between the bricks has flaked away, leaving deep undercutting of the bricks. This allows rain to penetrate into the wall, and frost will start to break up the bricks. The old, powdery, cement between the bricks has to be removed until firm cement is reached. This can be raked and brushed out, either with a special chisel or with some tool that fits the gap. Ready-mixes for repointing can be bought from a builders' merchant, or you can mix your own using three parts builders' sand to one part cement, and mix to a stiff texture. In the North, the mortar is trowelled in the gap between the bricks to make bricks and mortar flush, but in the South the mortar is cut back from under the top brick to present a slope to the weather. I think this looks better. Repointing is a job that can be done a little at a time, until this damage is repaired.

Christmas trees are usually thrown away or burnt on the fire, but if the tree has a straight trunk it can be a useful post or plant support in the garden, once stripped of its branches.

Flat roofs always leak and the place where the rain is getting in is always hard to find. Therefore never build, or have built for you, a flat roof. Even a very shallow slope on a roof will help. Save yourself expense and frustration.

When wiring a light switch, always run the live wire to the switch, not the neutral. It will work the other way, but current is still reaching the bulb-holder when the light is switched off, and it is not a safe practice, and I wish they would stop it. If anybody wants a pair of pliers with little round bits burnt out of the cutting edges caused by cutting live wires, I have a supply.

A slate that has come loose can be fastened back by getting a thin strip of copper 1 in (25mm) wide or even less, that is about the length of the slate, with a hole at one end. Pull clear the old slate and if it is not broken it can be used again. The slate you have removed lay on the join between two other slates, so look for the nails holding these slates down — that shows where the batten underneath lies. If the gap between the slates is tight, it will be necessary to drill a hole, using a masonry drill. Screw the copper strip to the batten, using a brass or stainless steel screw. Slide the missing slate back into place, lining up the end with the slates on either side, and then fold up the end of the copper strip to hold it in position.

If you want fine prints on your walls, haunt second-hand book sales and buy a few old art books. Then cut out the pictures that appeal to you and frame them. Fine art for the cost of the frame. In fact this is the source of most of the framed prints found in art shops, so you have just eliminated the middle-man.

The British Army has never stinted itself when it comes to tools. They have always bought the best, and now that the Army is shrinking, a lot of the tools are finding their way onto market stalls. These tools are the ones marked with an arrow stamped in the metal. Provided the tool has not been too heavily abused, an ex-Army tool will be the best of its type, and will last you a lifetime.

Many mechanics will say that an adjustable wrench is a clever device for smearing the corners off the head of a bolt, so that nothing will get if off. Despite this opinion, an adjustable wrench does allow you to move most bolts, without having to buy a whole set of spanners.

The paper with a thousand uses

You can make furniture from newspaper! Easier, though, are placemats — same principle. Roll sheets of newspaper really tightly and tie with string, looping very closely together to make something not unlike grass mats. If you use coloured magazine pages and roll them diagonally, you will get cheerful patterns.

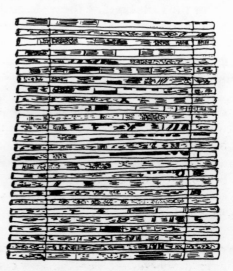

Make your own conservatory blinds by rolling newspaper tightly, tying with strong fine string and looping together for a 'grass mat' effect that will let light dapple into the conservatory. Penny pinching? Approximate saving: £990.

Too hot in the summer? Make a simple but very effective fan from pleated newspaper.

Papier-mâché is a wonderful, tactile medium with which you can make puppets, dolls, furniture for the dolls' house, or even, with some talent, boxes and furniture for people.

Maps, newspapers, cartoons — all can be used as wallpaper. It's only one step away from covering walls with posters, after all.

You can make a fun lampshade with newspaper. It can just be stretched around a frame and glued there, but you would probably be wise to use a low-watt light bulb. Another method, making a stronger shade, is to blow up a balloon and cover it with papier-mâché or with torn up squares and scraps of paper dipped in white glue. When dry, you can get rid of the balloon with a straight pin, and you have a firm lampshade.

Make paper hats out of newspaper for parties, Christmas crackers or even just for using while out in the garden.

When you're decorating, and want to get rid of old decals that children always seem to have stuck on their windows, soak them off with a little bit of vinegar.

Attractive bindings for towels, sheets, blankets needn't be expensive — just cut apart an old shirt or blouse, there are yards of strips there.

Old clothes can be turned into rag rugs, either braided or hooked or even crocheted — these are very economical for protecting your good carpets. When you're tired of them you can either wash them, relegate them to the pet bed or throw them away with a clear conscience, having pinched your pennies more than once.

Always have a supply of scruffy clothes ready to put on at a moment's notice. Otherwise, when an interesting job involving the bends in a soil pipe, or something leaking from under the car, has to be done, either you give up because it would ruin good clothes, or, more likely, you do the job, hoping to remain clean, and your hopes are dashed, yet again.

TAPE
SECURELY

Once you have made your own Christmas crackers you will probably never want another commercial one. About the only thing you will need to buy are the snappers themselves, and they cost only pennies from art and craft shops, and tiny toys if you wish. Everything else can be made, or recycled, or you will already have lurking in cupboards. Put all the little goodies, puzzles, rings and treasures onto the silly hat, roll them up or put them into little paper bags, and slide it all into the inner cardboard tube from a loo roll. Tape on the snapper, then put on the outside paper and trimmings.

Just because you cannot do all of a job does not mean that you cannot do any of it. If you want an extension on the house, you may know that bricklaying is beyond you, but that does not mean that you cannot find out how big a trench is needed and dig that yourself.

Things of plastic are notorious for little, vital, bits breaking off, and glues do not always work with plastics. If you have an electric solder iron the tip can be used to melt the plastic and fuse it back together.

Old election posters have their uses. The better sort of candidates have ones made of plastic and printed both sides, and these can be cleaned down and used on a work bench for assembly work requiring freedom from fluff and grit, say putting a carburettor back together.

Before spending any money on redecorating your house, it is a good idea to visit a few friends, and try to see their houses as though they were your own. Observe the cracks in the ceiling. Note the threadbare carpet. Their houses too have chipped paint and shabby corners that you never noticed before, because we are much harder on ourselves than we are on others. Now look at your house again. Do you really have to redecorate?

For the really belligerent screw that refuses to come out, first set a screwdriver in the slot and then hit the handle of the screwdriver with a hammer. This often frees up the screw and it can be taken out in the usual way. If it still resists, special bits are made that fit in a brace, and with that you can apply terrific power — so much so that it is easy to tear the head right off the screw. Then you have real problems.

'Neither a borrower or a lender be' is a sour-faced philosophy. It speaks of a dim-witted suspicion of your fellow man, which, for the most part, is unjustified. If often makes more sense to ask a neighbour if you can borrow a specialised tool, a hub-puller, say, than to buy one yourself. It is polite to return a tool on time, and if you try to ensure that it is in a better condition than when you borrowed it, you will find that people will lend. You should be willing to lend your tools, too.

DIY work pays: Example: for rebuilding a roof on a single garage, Quote £400. DIY job using best materials, £140. Example: neighbours' gate to back garden, done by local builder, £420. Mine to serve the same purpose and at least as effective, £23.

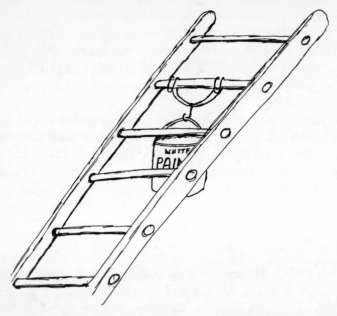

When painting on a ladder it is difficult to find a secure place for the tin of paint. Take an old coat hanger and squeeze the two arms together. Now bend these down about four inches (10 cm) from each end to make hooks to go over the rungs of the ladder. The paint tin hangs from the hook that went over the clothes rail.

We, the plodding foot soldiers of the DIY army, are pretty slow, and when we stop to work out how much we are saving for every hour of work put in, the answer is usually not very much. We may be saving only £1 an hour through our efforts, but if we would not be earning anything in that hour anyway, then we are £1 better off.

4
RECYCLING

Everybody knows about slicing rubber gloves into 'rubber bands' — wonder how many people actually do it?

Vegetable peelings go first into the stockpot. Then onto the compost heap.

Plastic net bags used for oranges and lemons make good scourers.

An old flush door makes a super sewing or work table span over two narrow chests of drawers.

When the plastic milk bottle is empty, and clean, cut off the corner at an angle to make a super scooper.

Use carrier bags as wastepaper bin liners, but if you use them in the kitchen waste bin, do make sure that they don't have holes in the bottom or slits where boxes have come through the plastic.

Save your old diaries for reference, and if you really want to get thrifty, you do know that there are only 14 different arrangements of the year, don't you? In theory you only need 14 diaries and 14 calendars.

Envelopes are perfect for filing anything and everything, especially the large ones with windows so that you can glimpse what's inside in case it doesn't match what you've written on the outside.

Map out of date? Turn it into a lampshade.

Save fabric remnants for quilts or mending, making children's clothes or craft projects.

Make a collection of well-designed initials, so often found in papers and magazines. Use for embroidery or drawings.

A piece of velvet or corduroy makes an excellent press cloth for pile fabrics, and isn't so painful as a needleboard.

Save yarn scraps, which can be knitted up into squares for blankets or for embroidery and tapestry or dolls' hair.

Zips are like buttons. Save them. Keep them organised. Use them again.

Transparent lipstick cases, cleaned out thoroughly, make a tiny housewife in purse or suit pocket.

Quilt interlining scraps can be used to make soft house shoes, using either sweatshirt or denim for the body of the shoe.

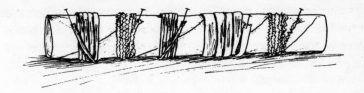

Keep ribbon neatly furled around a cardboard roll, and pinned down with a straight pin. You always need ribbon.

Cut apart an outdated dress and make it into an apron.

Sheets can be cut down for curtain lining. Curtain lining can be cut down for cot sheets. Cot sheets can be cut down for pillowcases. Pillowcases can be cut down for handkerchiefs. Handkerchiefs can be cut down for bandages. Bandages can be cut down for dustcloths. Dustcloths can be cut down for pot-pourri sachets. Pot-pourri sachets can be cut down for stuffing toys.

It is bordering on squandering money if you don't pass baby clothes — and equipment — around the family and friends.

If things are saved, they should be kept tidy and organised! It's no use hoarding something for seven years if, when it's just what you need, you can't find it and have to buy a replacement anyway. You KNOW you'll find the stashed one three days later.

Save any bit or piece of dowelling! Large for planting beans, small for homemade quilting frame, dolls' house or toy garage.

Use two jars for white spirit — one in which the brushes are first dunked, and when the sediment has settled, pour the clean spirit off into another jar which is for the next stage of cleaning. When the sediment has hardened in the jar, scrape it out and put in the base of a bonfire.

Save string. You can never have enough string.

Your own hair can be recycled. Either put it out for the birds to use in their nests or put it onto the compost heap, but don't throw it away.

An old piece of angle iron can be shaped into a tool which will remove dandelions and other deep-rooted, stubborn plants.

Tops of old music centres can make good propagators.

Re-use foil dishes, piedishes and so on in the freezer or oven.

Firelighters: Newspaper. Waxed milk or juice cartons. Candle ends. Anything soaked in a LITTLE paraffin. Dried orange, lemon or grapefruit peels.

Save magazines forever. Or burn them. Or cut them apart and file the bits of information you want. Or roll the pages to make 'grass mat' placemats with lots of colour. Or pass them on to someone else to read.

Have a toy circle in your circle of friends and neighbours.

Door knobs, drawer knobs, bed knobs. Save them all and mount them on a board on the wall, and you have a coat rack.

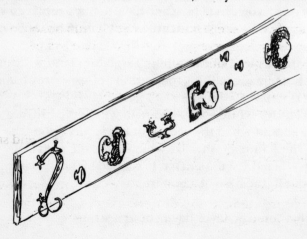

A piece of velvet makes a good record cleaner, for those of us who are old-fashioned enough to have a piece of velvet and records.

Bits and pieces of odd and broken jewellery are always useful — perhaps for the dolls' house, or for the dressing-up box.

Tightly-closing tins such as large instant coffee ones, golden syrup and baking powder small ones, make delightful toys for small children.

Recycle crayons — melt down in dariole moulds, mince pie tins or foil dishes in a warm oven while something else is baking.

Screw-top glacé cherry containers keep an 18-month-old quiet for four days. Also good for storing small toys.

Real keys on a real key ring — children love them.

Find a friendly packaging company, or printer, who has offcuts of card that they will give you. Offcuts can be a real problem for them, and they are a real gift to the penny pincher. Drawing and crafts become very inexpensive hobbies.

A perfect toy box: the sectioned wooden bulb boxes seen in garden centres and greengrocers'. If you have a tame greengrocer, ask him for one.

Carefully fold gift wrap and store in a box or roll it around a cardboard tube and loosely tie with a ribbon or string.

Save quizzes or riddles from papers and magazines and store them for using in Christmas crackers.

Egg white makes an excellent glue for paper. It is not a cheap glue for paper, though, if you break an egg just for the stickiness and then waste the rest of the egg.

Orange boxes from your friendly greengrocer can be transformed with a Stanley knife into dolls' house furniture.

Do your maths: you get more Christmas cards than you give presents, right? You could be swamped by gift tags cut from just one year's cards. But you can make bookmarks, postcards, scrap card, recipe file cards, spools for spare threads and ribbons, backings for photographs in a frame, bases for doing needlepoint lace . . . and finally they can warm you twice — once when you receive them, and again when you burn them.

Cut an empty plastic milk bottle in half. The top becomes a funnel, the bottom a handy portable mini-dustbin.

For fast dusting, or brass polishing, slip an old pair of socks over your hands. Rubber gloves dissolve in brass polish anyway.

'They say everything in the world is good for something' — Dryden. Even a discarded banana skin. The inside of the skin will clean patent leather shoes, and if you happen to own a donkey as well, you've made his day, it's one of his favourite snacks!

Tights or stockings make good strainers.

Towels which are past their best and about to join the cleaning/dust cloth pile are usually a bit unwieldy because of their size. Usually, though, there are only two areas that are badly decomposing, and with a nifty pair of scissors you can make several small washcloths, which are absolutely WONDERFUL for babies and small children — you need dozens of these (washcloths, not children).

Used A4 envelopes make good file folders, and a cardboard box makes a good file folder holder. You don't have to spend anything at all to have a good filing system!

Plastic bottles make superb moulds for candles, whether you are making new or recycled ones.

Charities sell stick-on labels which you can use on junk mail envelopes. Do not, however, try to use the postpaid ones if you're sending them elsewhere than to their original addressee.

Tights and stockings can be cut in a long spiral to make twine.

Patchwork quilts warm you in more ways than one — once when you're scrabbling among the fabric scraps to find the right colour, again when you're stitching it all together and it envelopes you, the table and the sewing machine, once more when you sleep under it and finally when you look at it and remember the dress made for a child who is about to be married.

Beautiful wool can be found in out-of-fashion sweaters, at charity shops and jumble sales. With a little bit of ingenuity and a lot of patience, you can unravel the wool, wind it into skeins, handwash and let dry, then wind into balls for re-knitting.

Tall, thin bottles make good rolling pins (it's all my mother ever used!).

Sell clutter. William Morris: 'Have nothing in your houses that you do not know to be useful or believe to be beautiful.'

Old leather belts or shoes can be cut apart to make leather washers or door handles for Morris Minors.

You can even recycle used engine oil. Keep a little for wiping over tools before you put them away — but DON'T keep oily cloths crumpled up in a corner, they can go up in flames if they get too warm. The rest of used engine oil should go to the municipal dump — there is NO EXCUSE WHATSOEVER for pouring used oil down a drain or in the street.

Save a few wine corks — you can stick them on the end of knitting needles to keep the dratted little stitches from sliding off the end, and they also make a nonscratch scourer.

If you learn nothing else from this book learn this: if you have children, do not deprive them of the greatest plaything known to mankind — the dressing-up box. Into this wonderful magic cavern throw all your outdated evening dresses and strippy-strappy heels, your cricket sweater and school jacket. Add ingredients for a magic show and kiss plastic toys goodbye because the children will find the real things a thousand times more fun. The box itself can be something recycled . . . our childhood one was a coffin case!

Eye up those curtains you're about to discard — they could be super teatowels or dishcloths.

Before you throw away an old chest of drawers, make sure that the handles or knobs aren't worth more than the chest! They could probably be used on a different chest, at least.

Shredded newspaper can be used instead of straw or wood shavings when stabling a horse. There is an added advantage that horses will not eat it.

Save all candle ends to melt down and make new candles, using plastic bottles, tins, whatever for moulds. However, you will have to buy new wick! Our first effort many years ago was a disappointment — the candles simply would not light! When we went back to the shop where we had bought the string we used, the shopkeeper explained that she wasn't surprised they wouldn't burn, as the string was meant for hanging pictures and was fireproof.

As coat hangers obviously breed and multiply in the wardrobe, new uses must constantly be found for them. In addition to sticking them into the car radio aerial hole, they're just right for barbecue skewers and for bending into a frame for holding clothespeg bags you've made — perhaps from old curtains.

Wood-burning stoves will burn almost anything that is burnable. They burn newspapers rather well, so if no other use can be found for your old papers, burn them in addition to wood or instead of wood. After all, paper is just processed tree.

Almost everyone who writes to us at the *Penny Pincher Paper* sends their letter in a reused envelope.

Making your own paper is both fun and inexpensive. You need a kit, or the ability to make a filtering screen, but after that there is no special equipment needed, just lots of scrap paper, newspaper and, for really special quality paper, some old rags. Notice on very good stationery the phrase 'high rag content'.

And here's how to use up slivers of soap: Collect enough slivers to equal about a bar of soap (you want them rather dry). Scrape away and discard any unsightly grey bits. Shred the slivers into any plastic container such as shaped bubble packaging, soap mould or similar pretty shape (sea shells work, too). Fill the mould to the brim, pack down, refill right up to the top, and then gently pour in warm water to the top. Leave to dry — several days — smoothing down the top from time to time. When completely dry, tip out and let dry hard. If you always buy different colours of soap you will have lovely marbled bars, which won't fall apart.

An outdated blouse or shirt can be cut apart and used for making underwear!

Not only are egg boxes just right for storing fragile Christmas ornaments, you can also MAKE ornaments from some kinds.

Beautiful dolls' house linens are made from old shirts and blouses.

Christmas tree decorations are not one of the essentials of life, so we spend very little on them. On the other hand, we never throw any of our decorations away, and we take off and store the tinsel for the next year — and the year after that. The result of years of accumulation is that our tree is usually described as 'gross'. The angel has been on the top of every tree since 1963.

5
GARDENING

As soon as wood ashes are cool, scoop them up and put them straight on to the garden.

Egg boxes make good 'peat pots' for starting plants.

If you're lucky enough to find wool-nylon mix yarn in green, it makes fantastic death-defying garden twine.

Plan ahead on your vegetable planting. Little and often with lettuces — gluts are hard to deal with. Choose varieties of vegetables to suit your family. If they hate broad beans perhaps they'll like French beans better.

Plant vegetables that will fill the Hungry Gap as well as your freezer. Fresh food from the garden is particularly welcome in those first lovely days of spring, and if you're harvesting things you aren't quite so tempted to plant too early.

Do you know about sprout sprouts? All the books condemn 'blown sprouts', but if you ignore the books and let your sprouts do just that, you will find an epicurean delight not unlike asparagus, at just the Hungry Gap time of year. Let the sprout-sprouts grow to about four or five inches long and then steam or lightly cook them.

Plant rhubarb.

The best bird-scarer is free, bio-degradable and very, very quiet. First, obtain a dead bird. Attach one leg to a branch with a piece of string, letting the wings and head hang down to flap gently in the breeze.

Next best bird-scarer is tape — either computer or cassette — wound around in a tree, or stretched between two sticks along a row — twisted as it's wound so that it pulsates with light reflections.

Jam jars or larger jars turned upside down over delicate plants make a mini greenhouse. Even plastic bottles can be cut in half and shoved in the ground to give plants a chance to grow before the slugs and snails pig the lot.

Do you grow broad beans? Do you let blackfly enjoy YOUR feast of beantops?

Corn-salad or lamb's lettuce is pretty, and thrives in the Hungry Gap. Let it develop its seed heads which add delicious crunch to early salads.

For early salads, you can mix together your leftover vegetable seeds such as lettuce, beetroot, spinach, parsley, or any other edible-leaf ones, and plant in a row or block for cut-and-come-again, or thinning and then letting, say, all the spinach that remains grow on to maturity.

Yogurt or instant-noodle cartons make super potting-up pots for young plants. Poke holes in the bottom with a skewer.

If you're cold in the garden, you aren't gardening hard enough.

Moles don't like noise. Any kind of noise — stamping, hitting the ground with a shovel, wind blowing across the necks of bottles inserted into their runs.

Invest in a water butt if you don't have one. Your plants don't need processed water.

Find work and gardening clothes at jumble sales. Ten pence for a sweater means less agony if you shred it than if you shred your Guernsey.

Cold tea really does make a good plant food — indoors or out — and tea leaves make excellent food for roses especially (is this why they're called tea roses?).

Plan your garden to be a gourmet one. It's a waste of space to grow something that's dirt cheap in the shops and then do without asparagus and artichokes.

Swap plant cuttings with friends. Swap. Not swipe.

Stretch the feet of tights or stockings around a circle of strong wire (clothes hanger, for instance). Secure with string and attach to a long pole for a handy fruit-picker, or a device for skimming off pond weed. Though don't forget that pond weed is actually an oxygenating plant. You may not like it, but the fish do.

Store bulbs in tights or stockings.

If you make hanging baskets, rake or scrape moss from your lawn or path . . . there always seems to be at least one damp, dank corner of a garden that nurtures moss.

Eggshells can be crushed and added to the compost heap, or steeped in water to make a liquid feed for lime-loving plants, or just added to acid soils.

95

Save your own seeds to supplement those that you buy.

So simple: you can actually save soap by using it! Before you go out gardening, scrape your nails along the bar of (recycled) soap, leaving no room for dirt to collect.

Cats don't like black pepper. Rotten onions work, too, and these can be obtained free from a greengrocer. Of course it might keep YOU out of the garden as well!

Old tights and stockings can be used for tying up plants to stakes so that they are not strangled.

There are only two sorts of plant: the quick and the dead. If a plant is malingering, it is a waste of space.

The garden is the penny pincher's sanctum sanctorum, the place to go instead of spending money on entertainment. All the world is in the garden.

Inside or outside, half a plastic bottle makes a superb cloche for plants — just don't try to fool yourself into thinking they're a Victorian bell cloche, they're half a plastic bottle.

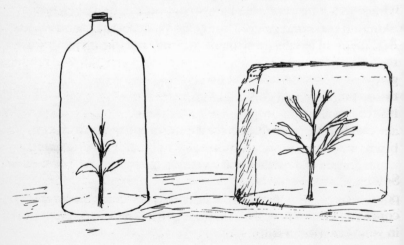

Cut yogurt or similar cartons into 'sticks' to use instead of buying plastic labels.

Washing-up water can be used on plants.

Avoid chemical weedkillers and pesticides like the plague. Not only are they potential people killers, they are exceedingly unkind to your wallet. If a packet of seeds only cost 50p, why pay £4.50 to try to save them from aphids? A little soap or detergent in a spray bottle works.

If you have carrot fly in your garden, don't try to grow carrots. Buy carrots from the greengrocer and grow something else in your garden.

A large old table fork (jumble sale, antique stall, car boot or charity shop) is a wonderful weeder.

Globe artichokes are delicious, and if you grow them yourself, they are free. Even better, they multiply, and their progeny are just as delicious. The plants are attractive, can even be grown alongside flowers, suppress weeds underneath them, and are diabolically difficult to dig up when their useful life is over, but it's worth it!

Another gourmet crop to grow oneself if there is possibly room is sweetcorn. The old saying is that you can walk to the garden to cut sweetcorn but you must run back to the kitchen to cook it, and if you ever taste really fresh corn you will know it's true. This is the crop besides swede that really is greedy about the room it takes, though, because you must plant it in a block, not rows.

Soft fruit, and indeed tree fruit, will save you hundreds of pounds over just a very few years, Grow your favourites, and consider yourself lucky if you have pears, cherries and quinces in your garden.

97

Even the smallest garden ought to have a few asparagus plants, just for luxury and the beauty of the ferns in flower arrangements. The real penny pincher will recognise the saving in growing one's own, and appreciate the quality of better living for less. After all, pennies should be pinched to make one's life better, not worse!

We have never succeeded in growing a bay, but stubbornly keep trying. Our last effort consisted of six or seven cuttings which were doing well in small pots on the patio until a gale left us with six or seven pots each containing a small neat hole in the middle of the compost. Try to grow bay, it is another penny pincher's necessity.

Horseradish will take over the world.

98

So will mint.

Perpetual spinach is a must. Grow a few plants of summer spinach if you like watching things bolt, but perpetual spinach will give you delicious beds for marinated chicken, generous quantites of puree on which to spread a strip of sorrel puree for a superb starter, and bowl after bowl of fresh salad. Excellent Hungry Gap plant when planted the year before, giving you early spring real food from the garden.

Marrows are another crop that varies according to when you harvest it — small courgettes, satisfying marrows, and if you can bear to forgo some of the fruit, the flowers can be cooked in batter, but this is rather like eating baby corncobs — why not wait unti it grows up and gives you more?

Turnips are a bit like sweetcorn — unless you've had them straight from the garden, you've been eating them à la Scarlett O'Hara — pithy and dry. The greens are delicious!

Keep at least one grape vine if just for its leaves. Greek dolmades, homemade, is one of the great dishes of the world, and very economical to make.

Ground elder was originally planted as a garden vegetable. Eating it is such sweet revenge.

Plan your gardening so that you have small amounts of many different vegetables coming on all the time — use your freezer for storing gluts of fruit, which freeze better than you can freeze your own vegetables, and are more expensive in the shops.

It's all a matter of preference, but years of experience have shown that the vegetables sheared off by a Dutch hoe easily outnumber the ones inadvertently beheaded by a swan neck hoe.

A garden without herbs is truly a garden without spice. Even the cheapest, meanest, most parsimonious meal can be lifted to gourmet tastes with the addition of home-grown herbs. Try some of the ones that don't package well, such as lovage, parsley, rosemary, lemon thyme, tansy. When you have your own sage plants you'll never want the dry, powdery, tasteless stuff in jars again. Toss a branch of rosemary or sage or even lavender onto the barbecue grill and sit back and wait for the compliments.

A fine lawn is a splendid thing, but it is expensive in time and money. It needs feeding and weeding and careful mowing and watering. A good, serviceable lawn can be much cheaper and less work. Moss can be controlled to some extent by letting the grass grow longer, and if daisies cost £5 a dozen we would pay a fortune to grow these charming little flowers in our lawns.

Time, as well as money, is to be spent wisely. Grass clippings left on the lawn feed the lawn, save your time and your money as well because you don't need lawn food. Grass clippings laboriously collected in a grass box or raked up and put onto the compost heap are a waste of time, as they will quite likely become yucky in the heap anyway. Frequently mown, the clippings will hardly show — otherwise you will find that there are lines of clippings. These can be lightly raked around or quietly ignored while you resolve to do the job sooner next time.

An old-fashioned grease band around fruit trees will collect little multilegged animals without poisoning everything else in sight at great cost.

Small plastic pots or deepish jar lids, filled with beer and sunk into the ground to their rims, are excellent traps for slugs and snails and do not endanger birds. Cover the tops with something — a slate rested on a stone or similar — so that rain doesn't wash out the beer. Empty out the dead drunkards every day or so and console yourself with the thought that they were very, very happy. Alternatively, go out at night snail-bashing.

Old window frames with most of the glass still in them make excellent cold frames.

A wooden pallet is just right for forming the base of the compost heap, allowing air to enter from the bottom of the heap. (A compost heap works exactly the same as a fire, you know.)

To make the surroundings for your compost heap, there is nothing better than four wooden pallets, and you can wire them together at the corners with coat hangers.

Salt makes a cheap and effective weed-killer for use on patios. Just make up a strong solution and pour on the unwanted weeds. Try to do this during a dry period, so that the salt has time to act before it is diluted by rain. Remember that salt doesn't differentiate between weeds and your treasured plants.

You can make all kinds of gardening tools for yourself — an old piece of angle iron can easily be made into a 'gadunger' for plunging into the ground beside a deep-rooted piece of unwanted plant life.

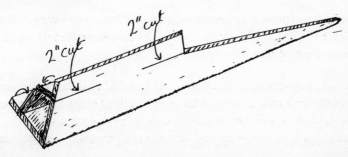

Before paying for manure from a stable or farmyard, ask around. Many stables have difficulty in getting rid of the stuff, and they will be grateful if you will take it away.

Fruit trees, if you have the land, are a good investment. They need little work and well-chosen trees will give more fruit than you can use. Here is where penny pinching is better than anything you can buy in the shops, because you can choose fruit trees for the best flavour, rather than weight of fruit, and most fruit loses some of its flavour between picking and selling.

Most garden machinery is bought by people who need it so that they can get through their gardening chores quickly, leaving them time to go down to the squash club to get the exercise they would have got if they had not used the garden machinery.

A rotavator is a mechanical device for chopping up weeds and distributing the pieces evenly around the garden in freshly-turned soil where they will prosper.

Power mowers may need servicing from time to time by a professional. Most of us wait until our mower does not start in the Spring before we send it in to be repaired, and the laws of supply and demand mean that the price of repairs at that time are at the maximum, and you will have to wait for the work to be done. The same job, done in the Autumn, will be cheaper, and you are in no hurry to get the machine back.

Nut shells can be used for mulch.

Laying a hawthorn hedge is easy. Cut the height of the stems to bridge any gaps in the hedge, and then saw or chop as near to the base of the stem as possible. The thinnest strip of bark will keep the hedge alive. Always lay a hedge so that the tops of the stems point up hill, and in towards the field. Any lengths of stem cut off can be used as stakes to strengthen weak points.

Forget about the twiddly bits at the top of the laid hedge. These look pretty, but are unnecessary. Wimps use gloves for this work.

If pests are eating your flowers or vegetables, heave on more manure. This will strengthen the plant and help it fight off the pest, and, even if that fails, there will still be enough of the plant for you and for the pest.

If you are making a vegetable garden in a lawn or old pasture, cut and remove any long grass, and then use a spade to cut through the turf to a full spit deep and turn it into the bottom of the hole. This will clear most of the weeds and the turf makes an excellent fertiliser.

Leaves, even the toughest like chestnut leaves, will rot down to make compost. Corral the leaves in chicken wire to make a heap four feet or more in height. It may take two years, but you will end up with a fibrous material that will do for peat.

Another way of clearing land to prepare it for planting is to cover it with a sheet of black plastic. Weigh the plastic down with stones and leave over winter. This will not kill the seeds, but it will get rid of the grass and weeds.

A garden incinerator will not only turn twigs that are too large to compost into ash phosphates, but it also lets you burn persistent weeds, such as dandelions and bindweed, that will lurk in a compost heap, along with the wood.

If you have to smoke, then grow your own tobacco. Tobacco grows quite well in the English climate, and the industry was only suppressed in the eighteenth century in order to protect the growers in our American Colonies.

When you do have a little sunshine on your seedlings, newspaper makes a good sunshade.

Newspapers can be added to the compost heap, but you should shred them first. They are the last things to rot down, so you don't want a high percentage in the heap.

For protection from the sun in the garden, you just can't beat a bonnet! Make one from an old shirt.

People who want manure want a few bags, while people who sell manure want to sell by the lorry-load. To keep everyone happy, get together with other gardeners and buy in bulk, each taking what they need. Once having tried the system, you will see that the same principle of cooperative bulk buying can be extended to other things. Cases of baked beans? Sacks of flour? Cases of wine?

6
TRANSPORT

New cars depreciate fastest in their early years, and it is said that a new car loses 25 per cent of its value when it is driven out of the showroom, because it is now second-hand. It makes sense for us, the penny pinchers, to take advantage of the vanity of the rest of the world, and buy our cars when they are a few years old, but still have a lot of trouble-free miles ahead of them.

Four-wheel drive vehicles are expensive to buy, compared to an equivalent two-wheel drive car, and they are hard on fuel. Very few people who buy them have a need for them or a place to drive them, and the last thing Britain needs is herds of motorised nerds churning up the countryside. If you have one, stick to the roads.

Cars that lose thousands of pounds of value, just because they are getting older, are a real pain. The way round this is to buy a car that is going to increase in value, instead of getting cheaper — that is, a classic car. The best investment we ever made was to buy an old E-type Jaguar when nobody wanted the miserable rust-buckets. It does cost to keep a classic car in running order, but they hold their value and they can be fun. The difficulty, if you intend to make money on an old car, is to know which heaps of today are going to be the classics of tomorrow.

It is hard for companies that import foreign cars to make money in the British market, especially with the low value of the pound. These companies make up for a low initial price of the vehicle by increasing the price of the spare parts. This can lead to large and unexpected repair bills, especially for someone buying an older imported car.

107

As in all transactions, cash is a wonderfully persuasive argument in the minds of sellers. With cash in your pocket to pay, do not be shy of making a seemingly low offer. Try to keep a straight face.

Second-hand cars loaded with extras are loaded with things to go wrong.

Work out whether you really NEED a second — or third — car or it's just that you WANT one. How many times in the last year have you been truly stuck without one? Could you have rented a car, or taken a bus or taxi? Which would be the cheaper alternative, the rental or the cost of running the second car?

More miles for your money

Petrol consumption increases sharply with increasing speed, so slower speeds may not save your life, but they will save your pocket.

Fast acceleration takes energy, and this energy has to come from the fuel. Slow, steady acceleration is much more economical.

Heavy braking turns the momentum of your vehicle into heat, which is then dissipated to the air. Then the car has to be accelerated again, using more fuel.

The above three tips may take all the fun out of driving, but you will save a lot in fuel bills.

There is precious little evidence that one petrol is better than another, so buy on price. This usually means the supermarket, and never means motorway petrol stations.

Fill up with petrol from a superstore or other cheaper source
(don't feel guilty — the same petrol companies are still making
their profit!).

Modern cars may be rather boring, but they are much more
efficient in their use of fuel than old cars. For sheer economy it
is hard to beat a small, modern car.

Heavy cars use more fuel than light ones, because it takes
more energy to pull a heavy car up hills. On the other hand,
heavy cars are likely to be safer in an accident than a light one.
You pays your money, and you takes your choice.

High performance cars driven hard need high performance
oils. For the rest of us, the £3.99 a gallon stuff is quite adequate.
It is much more important for the protection of your engine to
change the oil filter regularly, than it is to use expensive oil. I
know one man who did not change the oil in his car for
120,000 miles, just topping it up as required. He said it looked
like oil, smelt like oil, and felt like oil, and until someone
proved otherwise, it was oil. He has a point.

'If it ain't broke, don't fix it' can't be said too often. It is still a
good motto with all machinery.

Tyre sense

Do you know what the numbers and letters on the sides of tyres mean? Do you pay too much because you DON'T KNOW?

Tyre companies go to great lengths to persuade us that their tyre is the product of advanced engineering and, no doubt, at high speeds and under severe braking conditions, these differences are significant, but they are not going to make much difference to people who drive their cars for economy anyway. We, as customers, have to remember that companies that advertise heavily have to recoup the cost of advertising from us, so part of the cost of an expensive tyre is the cost of telling us how good it is. Shop around for the cheapest, British-made tyre, and remember to haggle.

Having bought your tyre, it will last longer if it is always at the right pressure (look in the handbook of your car to find that), and if the wheels are properly aligned.

Tyre pressure, either too much or too little, shortens the life of a tyre. Word of this economy seems to have got around, for it is now difficult to find an air pump at a garage that does not have a queue waiting. The temptation is to drive away, vowing to check the pressure the next time the car is filled up. It is better to get a foot pump with a built-in pressure gauge, and make sure the tyres are kept at the right pressure.

It is a waste to throw away a tyre that is still legal, but only just. That worn tyre can go in the boot as the spare, and then it is only used in an emergency and put back in the boot when the damaged tyre is repaired or replaced.

Your car is not going to last for ever, so good maintenance is about making it last longer, putting off the day when it has to be replaced or, if it must go, ensuring that it will go for a good price. With that in mind, we can now stand back and decide what repairs and maintenance are worth it, and what are not justified.

Unless your car is still under warranty and you are obliged to use a dealer garage, find yourself a good 'home-tune' mechanic who will come out and fix your car — they are generally very good at most makes, and exceedingly reasonable in price.

Check your car (or bicycle) every day, keep it in good condition.

Check that oil and water, make the time to do the tyre pressure — you're throwing money away if you don't.

Unless an oil leak is really bad, it is going to be cheaper to top up with oil a little more frequently than to spend money stopping the leak. Oil that is being burnt in the engine and appears as blue smoke from the exhaust is a different matter; that has to be repaired.

As cars get old, they become reluctant to start, so a pair of jump leads in the boot is a good investment. Provided you have the jump leads, some kind motorist will pull up beside you and help you on your way. You will also be able to help someone else who needs a start.

In an emergency, the foil used to pack cigarettes can be screwed up and used as a fuse in a car.

Tights and stockings make emergency fan belts for cars.

Before throwing away a leaking car radiator and replacing it with a new one, take it down to a radiator repair shop. They will strip out the damaged parts and the radiator will be as good as new for about half the cost of a replacement.

A leaking radiator far from a garage is a problem. If you try to drive to the garage, the engine may overheat and be ruined, while if you take the radiator off, you cannot get to the garage. A solution can be to put half a cup of porridge oats in the radiator. This will form a sticky, glutinous mass that will block a small hole until a proper repair can be done.

Anti-freeze not only stops your engine freezing in cold weather, but also stops corrosion so it is needed all year round.

Buy anti-freeze in the summer. As the temperature goes down, the price goes up!

Batteries now come sealed-for-life, so they need no servicing. The most common reason for having a flat battery is that we have left the lights on overnight, so it is worth while having a battery charger that can recharge the battery and get the car going again, without having to call out a garage.

Bodywork

If the mechanical parts of a car go wrong, they can be replaced by buying new parts. If the bodywork rusts, then the repairs will be done by hand, and that can be expensive. Good bodywork in a second-hand car is more important than good mechanical parts.

Rust never gets better on its own, and one day your car will return to rust. The sooner you act to stop rust, the cheaper it will be. If your car is showing signs of rust in the sills and other hard-to-get-at spots, try pumping Waxoyl, available from car parts shops, into the bodywork.

Cars come with pretty weather-resistant bodywork these days, so they can safely be left outside. This then frees the garage for setting up a workshop, where all those repairs that are going to save you money can take place.

You don't need expensive chrome cleaners for your car — a little bit of vinegar on a cloth, a clean and then a good rinse to get rid of the acidy remainder, and follow up by polishing with . . . newspaper.

Rainwater washes cars.

As in every other aspect of life, planning ahead saves money. How many journeys did you make in the car last week that could have been combined? Those little trips to get the paper and pick up more milk are the ones that give you the worst mileage and cause the most wear on the engine.

A roof-rack will let you carry home that chest of drawers you got at the sale, without paying a haulier. Since roof-racks are cheap this makes a good investment. Do not leave a roof-rack on your car when it is not needed, since the extra air turbulence cuts your mileage.

Towing brackets give you the flexibility to move heavy loads with your own car. When buying a new car the salesman will usually ask if you want one fitted, and the temptation is to agree. Since we are spending thousands on the car, a few hundreds seem insignificant, but the same towing bracket can be bought for half the price from a motor shop, and they are easy to fit. Towing brackets also protect your car from backing into walls, and from over-friendly cars behind you.

If you travel abroad do your own comparison-shopping between travel agents and airlines. It can sometimes save three-quarters of the fare if you simply spend an extra night in the country you're visiting!

If you live in the provinces and visit London, you can save money, time and temper by parking your car on the outskirts, taking the Tube in and travelling by Tube, bus and taxi while you're there.

If you regularly travel by bus, get to know your zone fares — it may be that you can get off a little bit early and walk the short distance that made the difference between one zone's cost and two zones.

Donkeys are wonderful beasts of burden — 1) they are beasts and 2) they are a burden. Sweet, lovable, cute, a virtual member of the family, but if you think for one minute that you can hang a couple of plastic carrier bags across their shoulders as panniers, think again.

Some animals will willingly trail a cart, a wagon, or sledge behind them, in which sit their happy owners and their goods and chattels. Some animals.

If you fly quite often, you are more likely than the average nailbiting, terror-stricken passenger clinging to the edge of the seat to be upgraded to first class when the bus gets full. This almost surely means that it's a big company which is saving money, not the average human being, but life's like that sometimes.

If only one person is travelling, say, into London from the provinces, it will probably be cheaper to do so by train. If two or more of the family are travelling together, it is much cheaper by car (unless, of course, you get a speeding ticket/parking ticket/get the car stolen, etc.).

Like airlines, trains have weird and wonderful pricing structures. The only thing that you can do is STUDY train times and ticket prices and do your best to travel at the times when tickets are reasonable. Haunt the wretched station manager's office, or if they have some little corner marked 'customer service', do not take this too seriously, but go and make them earn their day's salary.

When travelling on company business, stay at the best hotels and send in enormous expense claims. This will enhance your status. When travelling in Britain, or on the Continent for that matter, and you are paying for your own accommodation, save money by staying at bed and breakfasts. You never know what you will find, so they are always interesting, and that is more than can be said for most hotels. Breakfasts tend to be vast, and seem to consist of cholesterol with little bits of bacon and egg floating in it. Wonderful.

Much of the planet travels only by bicycle. Some countries are much better organised for cycles (Holland is wonderful!) but after taking your cycle proficiency test, you really ought to use cycles as much as possible. Just remember that you really don't own the road, and the motorists aren't going to be looking out for you, especially if you weave in and out of the traffic occasionally tagging a ride on the back of a lorry by hanging on to its rear corner.

If you are serious about saving money, and would like to feel better in the process, there is no better way of doing it than walking any reasonable distances.

Britain has the world's best network of public footpaths, quite unknown to unfortunate peoples across the Channel. Healthy and interesting exercise is within the reach of everyone, and at no cost. Your rights to a footpath are the same as those on a public road, but please shut gates and follow the Countryside Code.

A great yachtsman once told us: 'A boat is a hole in the water, surrounded by wood, into which you pour money.'

7
APPLIANCES

Keep a file for all the instructions for your appliances and similar household purchases. Staple the purchase receipt to the instruction booklet.

If all else fails, READ THE INSTRUCTIONS.

Learn how to diagnose faults when an appliance fails to work by first looking through the instruction booklet. You would probably face a call-out charge when the only problem might be, for example, that the cooker is on timed programme and therefore won't come on manually. I have had a wonderful washing machine repairman who kindly pointed out that my machine wouldn't pump out because it was perishing cold outdoors and the drains were frozen, and there was no call-out charge, but gems such as he are few and far between, believe me.

It is cheaper to boil water in a kettle than on the cooker in a saucepan . . . and the meter doesn't know whether you're going to make a cup of tea or boil peas.

Empty: vacuum cleaner bags, dryer lint traps, dishwasher strainers.

If you have night-rate electricity, invest in a programme-timer so that your appliances such as the washing machine actually work during those cheaper hours . . . if you (and your neighbours) can sleep through all the noise and you are happy in your own mind that you won't wake up to a plumber's nightmare.

Many people find that night-time cheap rate electricity works well for them, but remember that you have to have the life-style to make it worthwhile — everything you use during the day is charged at a higher rate than the normal domestic rate.

Before you call in the repairman for a noisy appliance, check that it is on a level surface. Even electric typewriters make a funny noise if they're not level.

Check the seals on all your appliances — if you can slip a piece of paper out of a closed door, the seal is not a good fit and money oozes out, whether the appliance heats or cools.

Cut your cooking costs

Make sure that bottoms of saucepans are flat to heat evenly and efficiently. If they aren't flat, fram the daylights out of them with a wooden mallet until they are.

When you have finished baking (having turned off the oven early, of course), open the oven door to let the heat out which is also better for the oven inside, as then the moisture doesn't condense. Be sure that small children aren't hovering too close.

Pressure cookers make wonderful stews in a fraction of the time taken on a cooker.

Use — or improvise — a steamer to cook two or three foods for the price of cooking one. The flavours do not mingle. Trust me.

Not so much an appliance, but an expensive pot: get the best and largest steamer you can afford, especially if you grow your own vegetables. You will often come in from the garden in the early part of the summer with small amounts of five or six different vegetables — what a feast, and how easy when they're all cooked in one pot so economically! But the feeling you will get is not that of being a miser, but a gourmet.

If there is boiled water in the kettle left over after making tea, many people put the excess in a vacuum flask to save for later.

Microwaves melt lipstick.

Make cleaning either the barbecue grill or the oven shelves easy, but BE CAREFUL WHILE YOU'RE DOING IT: wet a few newspapers, put the HOT grill or shelf on them, cover with more wet newspapers, and let the steam do the work. When the papers are cool, unwrap and wipe off the residue with them.

You won't need oven cleaners if you keep your oven clean all the time. Make it a habit to wipe it out each time while it's still warm — even if it's just with newspaper, it helps.

You can wipe out your oven with a bicarbonate of soda/water mixture to help keep it clean.

Water can be heated to boiling. Full stop. Once it has boiled, TURN DOWN THE HEAT. It doesn't get any hotter than that, and you will be wasting heat as well as evaporating the water you've boiled.

A dishwasher is a dishwasher, not a garbage disposal unit. Scrape the food off the dishes before loading — you do for the washing-up bowl — so that the machine runs efficiently and lasts longer.

Don't buy more technology than you need in appliances. If you have a dishwasher you will probably already know that you actually only use the 'rinse and hold' and 'wash' cycles — possibly two levels of wash — but I have yet to meet anyone who swans around their kitchen in high-heeled shoes choosing a third or fourth cycle.

Laundry economies

Use cold fill on your washing machine (you can get a small device to close off the hot tap for just a few pence). It costs less for your machine to heat only the water you're using, AND it gets the clothes cleaner. But you do need the Y-piece, which you can buy from a DIY or plumbers' shop because without it your washing machine will stop at the hot water cycle, and not all repairmen will tell you this for free.

If you soak clothes before washing, it will take less washing powder to get them clean. If you add a little vinegar or soda to the soaking water, it will take even less.

The wizard of the modern world is that wool cycle on the washing machine! If you have one, use it, rather than sending sweaters to the dry cleaners. Or wash them by hand.

Use your airing cupboard to dry laundry. Store linens in a chest or cupboard — any constant heat should be used for the best purpose.

Drying clothes takes expensive heat if it is done in the dryer. Using the clothes-line is the best way, for the sun and wind are free. In our unreliable climate it is useful to have an indoor place to dry things, and a ceiling airer can be made out of a broom handle and three old wooden hangers, plus lengths of 10mm dowel. Clamp the three coat hangers together and drill four holes through them, two near each end and two a quarter of the way along each arm, just large enough to take the 10mm dowel. Cut four lengths of dowel the same length as the broom handle. Slide the coat hangers onto the dowels, with one coat hanger at each end and one in the middle. Glue or pin in place. Now make three notches in the broom handle to match the coat hangers, about one-third the thickness of the broom handle. Drill the junction of the hangers and the broom handle and fasten with brass screws. A rope goes from each end of the frame to a pulley screwed into the ceiling joists and down to a cleat on the wall. Attach strings from the outer dowels to the lifting ropes, about 9 inches (23 cm) from where the ropes join the frame, to stop the frame from rocking. Now your clothes dry overnight for free.

Switch off your iron early. More delicate fabrics can still be successfully ironed using residual heat.

Work out wattage: Dryer 2500. Iron 1200. Now work out how long it takes you to iron five shirts. Let's say it takes you an hour (don't you just hate maths?). You will use 1200 watts. Five shirts in the tumble dryer will take about 20 minutes, or one-third of an hour, and 2500 divided by 3 = 833.333333333333 (aren't calculators great?) — 833 watts wins. Plus you have had 58 minutes' free time.

If thick, 'luxurious' towels have started to pong because it's devilishly hard to get them dry, put them through the washing machine using Dettol or similar instead of washing powder. When the wash is finished, run them straight back through on a normal wash with washing powder and either a fabric softener or white vinegar as a rinse. Works on anything.

Put your fridge or freezer in the coolest possible place, not adjacent to the central heating boiler!

A freezer is a money-saver! Even if you don't grow your own vegetables and fruit, it means you can take advantage of pick-your-own, of bulk buying and special offers from butcher and greengrocer. It also means you can shop less often, thereby saving transport costs and time.

A full freezer is more economical to run than an empty or half-empty one. This is no problem for those who grow their own fruit or vegetables, but for those who don't, fill empty plastic containers with water and fill all the empty space in the freezer.

Know what you want to get out of the refrigerator or freezer before you open the door.

Keep your refrigerator and freezer organised and tidy so that you don't stand gawping at the inside while you let the cold air (which cost you money) swirl outside, neutralising the warm air (which probably cost you money), and the warm air whoosh inside . . .

To make defrosting a chest freezer a little bit easier, put several layers of newspaper in the bottom when you've emptied it, and you can empty out newspaper, frost and water all in one go.

One of the most marvellous, money-saving modern devices we have is a bag-sealer. Maybe not so modern — we bought it in 1975 — and use it for the freezer all the time. It's also great for re-sealing big bags of bought frozen food, and will usually work on other packaging, including cereal bags. It would be difficult to calculate how much this one appliance has saved us in twenty years — dare I say it? — without one second's trouble. Congratulations to Bosch.

Heating control

If you have central heating, watch the bill like a hawk!

Turn down the thermostat, make sure you can control the radiators. Individual controls for each radiator are one of the best investments you can make for economy. This can't be repeated too often.

Turn down the temperature on the water heater, even if by only one or two degrees.

Use fewer hours on timed water heating — experiment until you can ACTUALLY notice a difference or everybody moans.

For fireplaces: stretch your fuel by making newspaper logs. You can use a log-roller, but you don't have to have one — just roll the papers good and tight, and wedge them into a box to help keep the shape. If you have plenty of free string, tie the rolls. It still seems illogical, but they don't unroll in the fire — they look even more loglike as they burn.

Everybody has their favourite way of making firelighters from newspapers — don't they? Roll them, scrunch them, fold them, twist them, but don't just throw them away!

Take advantage of any free wood. (Ask the farmer about the fallen tree before you haul it off.) Another source of free wood is from woodworking shops. Chances are they'll be grateful if you take away their waste wood, which can be a problem for them, a godsend for you.

If you use coal, do make up briquettes with the coal dust and a tiny amount of cement and water.

Eliminate draughts by covering unused fireplaces. Just leave a ventilation area so that air can circulate in the chimney and room.

Stuff balls of newspaper in draughty, unused chimneys — not in ones you're using, though!

Keep out draughts with a good, old-fashioned sausage, made from the sleeves of an old shirt, stitched together and filled with old tights and stockings.

Double layers work at windows, too. Curtain linings make a tremendous difference, particularly if they're hung on separate hooks from the curtains themselves, trapping warm air in the space.

Curtains hung over draughty doorways keep the heat in and the cold out.

If you have radiators, you can put foil behind them to help reflect the heat, and a shelf over radiators both deflects the heat into the room and helps prevent dark heat marks on the wall. But do put up the foil before you fit the radiators — it's difficult afterwards.

A hot water bottle is cheaper than an electric blanket. Have you ever had a hot salt pillow? (This is superb, by the way, for earache.)

Multifuel heaters are truly that. We watched in fascination as an acquaintance threw an old Wellington boot into the flames!

A fax machine is not only fun, it saves you money! You can transmit a page of information in two minutes that would take fifteen minutes over the telephone; if faxed you are only paying for the two minutes it took to transmit over the phone lines.

Unless urgent, you can wait to send your faxes until after 6.00 p.m. and take advantage of the cheaper rate.

Cats make ridiculously expensive mouse traps, but their cost looks more reasonable if they are classified under Entertainment.

8
FOOD

Make penny pinching fun. You will save money by planning your menus, so why not plan a month at a time, rather than just a week? Make that a trip-round-the-world month. Have Italian-style meals one week, Australian another, Russian the third and American (North or South) the fourth. Go to the library and you will find super cookery books — pick and choose the dishes you can cook with home-grown ingredients. You will know on the 4th of the month whether you will need rice on the 29th of the month. If you won't . . . don't buy any.

Offer your guests homemade cocktail snacks: potato skin crips. Cheese balls. Marmite sticks. Nuts and bolts.

No mushrooms? Use carrot slices instead — crunchy, cheap, especially if you grew them yourself.

Remember that the cheaper cuts of meat are just as nutritious as the expensive ones. You are NOT depriving yourself or your family of nourishment by choosing cheaper cuts.

Don't be afraid to be adventurous! If chicken is on special this week and you had planned a dish of pork, you can probably substitute the chicken in the recipe.

Use evaporated milk for cooking, diluted generally, as is for 'cream'.

Use less flour for coating meat by measuring a small amount into a paper or plastic bag; then add the meat and shake.

Make your own junk food snacks, they are delicious!

131

A beer bottle is a superb meat tenderiser. Hit the meat directly, not at an angle, with the small open end.

Use food tins to steam foods — especially if you have small amounts to cook. You can even throw them away after you've used them once.

Anything from a bottle of ginger ale to drained fruit syrup or leftover desserts can be frozen to make ice lollies or 'ice creams'.

If cornflakes have become limp, they can be crisped in an oven (while something else is baking). Or use them as a casserole topping.

You can re-use coffee grounds by baking them for half an hour or so in a moderate oven (you know I'm going to say it) WHILE SOMETHING ELSE IS BAKING.

Make your own beer.

Mix your own muesli, and add extra oats to bought muesli.

Buy a bag of economy frozen peas rather than eye-straining petit pois.

Make a batch of fudge, or clotted cream fudge (you use good old Carnation instead of cream), or toffee.

Substitute a casserole for steaks or chops; it will probably extend to two meals.

Add the last bit of a meat loaf to a tin of tomatoes for a pasta sauce, giving you a whole extra meal.

Just because a tin of anchovies has ten fillets in it doesn't mean you have to use all ten in the recipe specifying a tin of anchovies. Use fewer — say half — and the other half can be used a day or so later in another recipe. Keep the remaining half covered (tightly) in a dish, not the tin, in the fridge. Don't let them rot there.

If you are pouring all the cream from a container — say for a recipe — let ALL the cream drain out.

If you always keep a little rice and pasta in the cupboard, it won't be a disaster if you then forget to buy potatoes. And doesn't a still, quiet little voice deep inside you tell you that rice lasts longer than the 'best before' date on the packet? Read what it says: BEST before, not throw it out the day after that date.

Don't limit your pickle-making to chutney. Go to the library if necessary for a cookery book, but homemade pickles should be unique every year.

Homemade water biscuits or oatcakes are special.

Line the bottom of the salad drawer in the fridge with newspaper or paper towels to help keep vegetables fresher longer.

Freeze tomatoes. You are more likely to use them in stews and casseroles than you are in all that chutney. All you have to do is wash them, dry them and put them into bags. When you're ready to use them in cooking, throw them in still frozen, and they'll thaw as they cook.

Reduce stale bread to crumbs. Freeze only what you will actually use in a reasonable time — feed the rest to the birds, for goodness sake!

'Convenience foods' are always more expensive than conventional, and conventional ones are more expensive than homemade or homegrown.

'Empty' sauce bottles often have enough left to dilute with water, milk or vinegar for an extra serving or more. Add to dishes being cooked.

You don't have to have greaseproof paper, you know. Brown or white paper, brushed over with whatever oil or fat you're using, works as well now as it did for decades, unless of course you're going to sell the product, in which case you have to stick to all the commercial food regulations. And if you want the most delicious ham you've ever tasted, do it as they did in the Old South: bake it inside a heavy brown paper bag, then remove the bag, take off the skin, and score the fat into diamonds. Put a whole clove into each diamond, cover the lot with a mixture of brown sugar and American mustard, and pop back into the oven for about 20-25 minutes to glaze.

Loose tea is cheaper than tea bags.

Apple peels are edible. Cooked apple peels are still edible.

When you've melted chocolate in a SMALL saucepan, don't rinse it out. Let it dry and then scrape it out for chocolate decoration.

You can stretch your coffee by adding roasted, ground soya beans. The roasting, however, adds to the cost of the product because you need quite a high heat. The beans smell wonderfully coffee-like when they're done, but the initial whiff when they start warming is not coffee-like. You can also add ground chicory root to coffee — the French do this.

Leftover egg yolk is maddening — either plan to have scrambled egg with extra yolk straight away, or put the yolk into a small container and cover with water. Keep in the fridge, preferably only one day — otherwise it lurks.

You can make gravy out of nothing: using Cookeen or lard, melt the fat in a heavy frying pan. Add flour and let it brown — not beige, brown. Add hot stock (made with a stock cube or the real stuff), a sprinkle of herbs, stir until it resembles gravy.

Yesterday's leftover salad becomes today's pureed soup.

'For a delightful luncheon . . . slivers of leftover roast pheasant on thin brown bread . . . a wedge of pale crisp lettuce with blue cheese dressing . . . a succulent fresh peach, with a glass of cool, clear Sauterne . . .'

135

To keep lettuce fresh longer, rinse it still on its stalk, shake it as dry as you can and then keep it in a plastic bag in the fridge. Of course this isn't something you have to do if you've grown your own lettuces, you're usually trying to think of some way to use up several at a time.

Broccoli is edible. Broccoli leaves are edible. Broccoli stalk is edible. Broccoli flowers are edible.

Did you know that cooked lettuce is delicious? Not only leftover salad boiled and whizzed into soup, but deliberately cooking the lettuce from scratch! Our favourite way with lettuces about to bolt — or indeed, already bolting — is to put them into a casserole dish, add a little hot stock, cover the dish and BAKE them for about 20 minutes.

Jumbo oats, the really jumbo ones, make a reasonable substitute for chopped nuts in recipes. Toast them first.

Rice is reheatable, so don't throw leftover away — just rinse it well, and gently reheat in its own steam.

Check the price of loose bacon at supermarket delicatessen counters or at the butcher's — it is usually cheaper than the plastic-wrapped packages at the bacon display.

If you have never made your own sausages you are missing a lot! Delicious made into links, but not half bad just as sausage patties. Varieties are almost endless, and you know what goes into them!

Why buy cooked meats such as chicken loaf or even salami when it's so easy to make your own? If you can make a meat loaf, you can do it.

You really can store a cut onion on a saucer, with a bowl turned upside down to cover it.

If you do a lot of baking, you may find that a real (and expensive!) vanilla bean is a bargain — fill a jam or coffee jar with sugar, and bury the vanilla bean in it. The sugar will be vanilla-flavoured, and you just keep refilling the jar with sugar. For years.

You can freeze leftover bits of things like tomato puree, but you will probably just lose tiny packs of unidentifiable gunge down the innards of the freezer. It's much better to plan ahead, and be sure you use the second half which you've stored in a small dish or jar in the fridge before it gets black and hairy.

Homegrown tomatoes are SO delicious. You do know, don't you, that you wrap them individually in newspaper and stack them in greengrocers' boxes to ripen over the autumn, and you will almost surely have your own fresh tomatoes for Christmas dinner. Alternatively, fling them into the freezer the minute they ripen, to be added to stews and casseroles for fresh tomato taste. Don't expect to have frozen tomato nicely sliced for salad, though — they just won't cooperate.

Like the vanilla bean, you can grate orange or lemon rind and add to sugar. This is delicious for making biscuits if you remember to do it about a week beforehand.

When you have stewed fruit, use the leftover juice. By simmering for a little while you will have a little bit of jam that can be stored in the fridge — it will thicken a bit more as it sits there.

'You eat with your eyes first.' Hmmm. Eyes tend to have expensive tastes. If you're a chef or caterer, you will probably want decorated, lavishly-presented food — that's what people are paying for. If you're a penny pincher, you want delicious, satisfying food, and that's what you usually get by making it yourself. It doesn't need expensive 'dressing up' to be appetising.

Make your own bread, and discover how it ought to taste.

Jam-making has an undeserved reputation for being tricky. It's a piece of cake, and a real illustration of living better for less. If you haven't grown your own fruit, go and pick some. Wash it, weigh it, put it in a pan. Now add HALF its weight in sugar. Yes, half! Depending on how juicy the fruit is, you can add a little bit of water, but don't drown it, you only have to boil it off again. Now mash the fruit and simmer the lot until it's thickened — it will look slightly transparent, i.e. it will look a bit like jam! Do not fiddle around with thermometers or pectin or skimming away any of your jam — it's all edible — or paraffin wax or anything else you have to go out and buy. Just put the stuff into jars. Now the small print: make small batches at a time, and store in the refrigerator. Put the rest of the fruit into the freezer to make more small batches during the year.

Not everybody on the planet has a refrigerator. It is quite possible to live to a ripe old age without ever having had one — otherwise none of us would be here now, would we? If you need to keep something cool and the fridge is bulging to its seams with food — say at Christmas time when we all try to empty the food shops — and outside is too cold, think of the wine cooler! All you need to do is surround it with cold water. In a sweltering hot climate, milk — unpasteurised, unhomogenised, unirradiated, natural milk — is kept fridge-cool by putting it into a demijohn, tying a rope around the handle and lowering it into the water well.

Somehow pastry never fits the piedish. Even if it does we feel compelled to trim the edges and fiddle around making patterns. Since the oven will be hot, either fling a little bit of jam on scraps of leftover pastry or add some grated cheese to make straws, but DON'T put that pastry into fridge or freezer thinking you'll make something later. You won't, you'll waste the pastry. Do it now, while the oven is ready.

Pasta is one of the great foods of the world. It is user-friendly, compatible with just about anything, satisfying, inexpensive, long-lasting and a real budget stretcher.

A delicious way to cook sausages — or even other meats — and keep them from shrinking: put them into a frying pan with a little water (hot or cold), COVER the pan and simmer. Now watch them carefully and let the water evaporate, and the sausages brown.

When eggs are expensive, learn to use substitutes in baking: a smaller egg will make precious little difference in a recipe.

More egg substitutes: 1 teaspoon of vinegar = 1 egg, as does 1 teaspoon cornflour plus a bit extra water. So does an extra half teaspoon of baking powder. Soya flour is another substitute which is most useful. Use 1 tablespoon soya flour, 1 tablespoon water. Custard powder can be used in the same way — it's mostly cornflour anyway.

Don't throw out bacon fat. Save it in the same way as chicken fat. (see next page)

139

You can use the paper butter or marge wrapping to line your cake tins. Make sure the printed side is not next to your cake mixture, though — the ink will certainly be of food quality, but it just might mark the cake.

If you have a liquidiser you can make your own castor sugar.

You can also make your own icing sugar, but add a little cornflour to keep it from being sticky — it never seems to be so fine as bought icing sugar, anyway, but saves a trip to the shop if you find yourself short.

Make your own yogurt, by starting off with a spoonful of natural yogurt added to heated milk. You don't need lots of expensive equipment — a wide-mouth vacuum flask will do the job — or you can even just let it sit on the worktop in a jar until it 'yogs' and then put it in the fridge. If you want it as thick as the commercial kinds, add some milk powder when you start. Remember you're aiming for homemade yogurt, not commercial yogurt.

Honey is a super substitute for sugar — especially or perhaps only if you have your own beehives. In baking, remember that honey is about 25 per cent water, so for every 8 ounces (250g) of honey replacing 8 ounces (250g) of sugar, omit 2 ounces (50g) of liquid in the recipe.

When you bake a chicken, SAVE the fat. Pour it into a small container such as a ramekin, cover and store in the fridge. It lasts for weeks, and is delicious in cooking.

Save every bit of fat from all meats. A mixture of fats makes perfectly good shortening and cooking fat. Save expensive butter and olive oil for special purposes.

Learn how to render fat and clarify it. Don't let fat scraps sit around to become rancid — they're useless then. Even birds reject rancid fat. The easiest way is to put the scraps of fat into a tin, such as a cake tin, and put into the oven while something else is baking at a moderate temperature. Pour off the melted fat as it accumulates, into a suitable storage jar. Keep in the fridge.

To clarify fat which has sediments in it, simply add water, bring to boiling to melt all the fat and let it cool. Skim off the clean fat which will have risen to the top and solidified.

Vegetarians avert your eyes now. The average person needs about four ounces (100g) of meat per day, and this is enough, you don't have to eat the whole animal at one sitting. Meat is one of the most expensive elements of the food budget, but don't let vegetarians convince you that they live all that cheaply, because they seem to spend a FORTUNE on supplements, pills, vitamins, minerals and all those things that God so thoughtfully provided in meat. (And He added meat-eating teeth in our mouths, as well.)

Rabbit is delicious. Pigeon is delicious. Anyone who lives in the countryside already knows this — the information is here for townies. It is difficult to see why one shouldn't eat rabbit and pigeon, because rabbit and pigeon will do their utmost to eat everything in one's vegetable garden.

Keep a store of tinned and dried milk. Use them in cooking and baking, and keep the more expensive fresh milk for drinking and using in tea and coffee. (Hint: you can add more water than the diluting directions suggest.)

Make your own sour cream by adding a little lemon juice to single cream. Or a little vinegar. Stir in a bit of milk powder to make it thicker.

To keep from wasting things like biscuit dough, pasta dough, pastry by re-rolling and throwing away scraps from around the circles you cut, don't cut circles — cut squares.

If biscuits have gone limp, a few minutes in the oven will revive them. Preferably while something else is baking, otherwise it could be cheaper to buy more biscuits!

Any leftover meat or fish can be turned into pâté with the flick of a switch on a food processor, or the turn of a handle on a mincer. Add a bit of butter, a dash of cream if there is any, some imaginative flavours with herb, spice or bottle, a final slurp of alcohol if there is any.

A barbecue doesn't have to be an expensive steak or chop affair — belly pork makes a wonderful meal, with a sprig of rosemary or sage on the fire if you grow your own herbs.

You don't need eggs in coating batter — the lightest, crispest batter is made of just water and SELF-RAISING flour.

Stretch eggs with milk or water when you have scrambled eggs or omelette, they're lighter that way.

Make one orange go round six kids: wash, cut in half, remove pips. Cut into five or six pieces, put into the food processor with plenty of cold water. Whizz. Strain for real orange squash! This, incidentally, is perfect for adults, too, to send them on their way after a dinner party.

To serve only expensive food and wine at a dinner party is to confirm what your guests suspect: that you have no imagination.

There is a theory that if you buy smaller plates, you will then serve up smaller meals and people won't particularly notice. We bought smaller plates, and now have messier tablecloths than before.

Especially if you live in the countryside, you really ought to keep chickens for at least a year or two. You will know how a fresh egg ought to taste, you will learn that about 50 per cent of the chicks are male and therefore exceedingly delicious, and you will never, ever feel soppy about a fox again.

Don't bother freezing eggs. You have to separate them, then add either sugar or salt to the yolks, you'll NEVER get a foolproof system of marking, and the dratted little packages slither to the bottom of the freezer anyway, to join the infinitesimally small plastic blob of yellowish red greasy crevassed leftover spag bog that was to have been a midweek lunch if you could just have found it before you got frostbite.

Penny pinchers eat beans. Penny pinchers eat well! If you have never tried home-baked beans, find yourself a recipe (or write to us and we'll send you ours) and try them. Almost difficult to put a price on them, especially if you have a Rayburn or Aga and the heat is there anyway.

It is quite permissible to buy Sainsbury's dry sherry and pour it into a decanter to serve to guests. It is not permissible to buy Sainsbury's and pour it into a Tio Pepe bottle to serve.

If you are pinching pennies, there is no reason why your pets should live high off the hog. Downgrade their food as well, they won't starve. Pets lived on leftover scraps for most of history — they will even eat porridge . . . eventually.

Learn to love soup, and have one meal a week which is 'scrap soup' — all those tag ends of celery, carrot, leftover sweetcorn and peas, even bacon rinds.

Make your own wine and beer

Homemade wines are a cheap and efficient way of getting drunk.

Nearly all fruits and most vegetables can be fermented, but some give better results than others.

There are many recipes for making wines, and by all means stick with the one that works for you. Otherwise, for five gallons (23 litres) of wine, use 25 lbs (12.5 kilos) of fruit, chopped up, if it is hard, like apples, or mashed, if it is soft, like raspberries. Use a plastic, five-gallon (23-litre), brewing bucket, and put in the chopped or mashed fruit. Pour boiling water over, until the fruit begins to float. Make up a sugar solution of 15 lbs (7.5 kilos) of sugar and 1.8 litres of water, bring to the boil and boil for one minute. Watch carefully, for boiling sugar is very hot and it can suddenly boil over. Pour this in on top of the fruit. Put on the plastic lid and leave to cool. Make up a wine yeast as directed by the instructions. I use a wine yeast called Formula 67 that seems to be able to ferment anything from bilberries to boiler-plate. When the fruit and sugar mixture has cooled to blood temperature, add the yeast. Snap the lid hard down. The yeast will make carbon dioxide, and this, in a day or two, will force up the lid a bit. Leave it like that. The gap will be large enough to let out the gas, and the flow outwards will stop unwanted moulds getting in. Leave to get on with it in a warm place. Any time after six weeks, strain off the liquid into five demijohns and top up with water to make up the gallon. Fit an air lock, or cover the neck with a piece of cloth. Leave the demijohns until all bubbles have stopped rising. Filter, if you have a filter kit, otherwise strain through an old, but clean, pair of tights. Bottle in old wine bottles, and cork. Label the vintage with sticky labels. Store bottles on their sides. Homemade wines will go on improving for years, if you can wait that long.

Fruit, especially fruit like apples, can often be had for free if you see the fruit dropping off the trees, and you ask for it. It would be polite to repay your kind benefactor by giving him a bottle or two.

Books on wine-making at home make a great thing of cleanliness and sterilising, but this is not necessary. Ordinary home cleanliness is sufficient.

The cost of the materials, including sugar, to make 40 pints (23 litres) of beer from a beer kit is less than 20p per pint. This compares favourably with the cost of a pint in a pub.

Ginger Beer. To start, mix together 1 teaspoon yeast, 2 teaspoons ground ginger, 2 teaspoons sugar, in ¾ pint (450 ml) warm water. Stir and leave for 24 hours in a jug covered by a cloth. Every day, for seven days, add 6 teaspoons of ground ginger and 6 teaspoons of sugar. Then strain the mixture through a fine cloth. To this, add 1½ lbs (750g) sugar dissolved in 2 pints (1 litre) hot water, and the juice of 2 lemons. Dilute with 5 pints (2.8 litres) of water and put into 2- or 3-litre plastic bottles with screw tops. Every day, for seven days, loosen the top to let off the pressure. At the end of seven days, the ginger beer is ready to drink. When opening, remember that the top should be eased off, to allow for any build-up of pressure. The plastic bottle will not burst under even the most extreme pressure, but it is rather amusing to see the unwary after they have whipped the top off. Keep in the refrigerator and drink within two weeks. It is virtually non-alcoholic.

School lunches in our village school cost £1 a day. This is an opportunity to experiment to see how exotic a meal you can prepare for 50p.

Plastic lunch boxes for the children look good for the first week, but then the catch breaks. With a cheerful piece of cloth some wadding or foam rubber, you can make a lunch bag tha will be the envy of your child's schoolfriends.

Faddy eaters are a real pain and expense. Our rule is that children are allowed one food they can refuse, and after that they can eat up or shut up, and no snacks. My own rule is tha I will at least try any food that is eaten by men who wear trousers. If they wear sarongs or grass skirts, I will reserve judgement, but otherwise I will have a go.

During periods of penny pinching, can you put your hand on your heart and say you don't still buy CORNFLAKE Or crisps?

Use newspaper as a substitute for paper towels when you hav to mop up spills or absorb grease.

146

Vinegar in cooking

You can tenderise meat by soaking in water to which a little bit of vinegar has been added. This is often used for venison and other game, to make them a bit milder in taste and tender in texture.

A reasonable substitute for wine in cooking is a little bit of vinegar added to tomato puree and water.

If you have dried peas or beans which take an age to cook and are still tough, use a little bit of vinegar in the soaking water.

When you've picked your hops or herbs, hang them in bags made of tights or a sleeve from an old shirt.

A 28 lb (12 kilo) bag of potatoes from the supermarket – £4.25. A 56 lb (25 kilo) bag from the local farm shop — £4.00.

Baby food is a fine commodity, since it comes in convenient packages and takes no preparation. Just the thing for baby on a long journey. For baby's meals at home it is much cheaper and better for the child to use a mixer or dice the food you eat. This gets him used to your food, rather than the tastes of the commercial stuff. Go easy on the vindaloo, though.

Turkey is a festival food, but it is also cheap, so if there is a family festival coming up, serve turkey.

9
CLOTHES

Never throw away or recycle a garment before removing and saving the buttons.

Make tiny spools from spirals of card, save those last yards of thread in a pretty box and keep for repairs.

Darn that pair of socks as soon as there's a hole in one of them.

At a jumble sale, look carefully at how a garment is made — is there enough fabric in a full gathered skirt to make a shirt and trousers for a child? The important thing to search out is a skirt with only one centre back (or front) seam. Carefully removed from the waistband, you will find a generous stretch of fabric. Cost for shirt and trousers for a three-year-old girl, including buttons as well if you're lucky: around 10p.

You can make everything you wear — sheer tights and outdoor shoes would present a problem, admittedly, but other than that you are only limited by what you want to make.

Put on a pair of cotton gloves before you put on a sheer pair of tights to prevent snagging.

Old-fashioned but wonderful: thermal underwear.

Insoles, especially thermal ones, make enough difference to your foot comfort to merit going out and buying them! You can also make them from several layers of newspapers, though these tend to wrinkle — but then they cost nothing to replace.

Get to know your local shoe repair man.

When you have bought a new pair of tights, you can make them last longer by a little attention BEFORE you ever wear them: it is said that they will last longer if you freeze them overnight; one doesn't know why, but since it doesn't cost anything it's worth doing.

Another process said to prolong the life of your tights is to wash them before you wear them, preferably by hand. Use soap, not detergent. Plunge the tights into lukewarm water, getting them completely wet. Rub the soap onto your hands, not directly onto the tights. Get a nice sudsy lather, and gently wash with a squishing, not rubbing, motion, rinse thoroughly, blot with a towel, and let dry naturally.

Thick tights — unless they hurt in tight shoes — are truly 'warmer tights'.

Wash tights or other delicate clothes in a bag . . . made from old tights.

Hang lavender, etc., in tight-bags in the wardrobe.

Wear the panty part of tights (the legs of which you've cut away for other uses) as 'thermals' over ordinary underwear.

Stiletto heels are an ugly fashion, the cause of sprained ankles to the wearer, and damage to all types of flooring. The use of stilettos should be restricted to Sicilian bandits.

Never throw away an old T-shirt! Dust cloths, cleaning cloths, shirts for smaller people, strips and bits sewn together to make enormous, long snuggly nightgowns, strips cut off the sleeves to make headbands. Blessings to the person who invented T-shirts!

Vegetable dyes work on fabrics. To make a really permanent one, you need a mordant to fix the dye, so off to the library for a book about it, because one doesn't work for them all, it's a whole speciality subject. Fun, though, for making your own yarn rugs.

Mend holes in your pockets the minute you see them!! Money falls out of holes in pockets.

Protect seldom-worn clothes in the wardrobe by putting an old shirt over them.

Never throw away a jacket just because the lining has given up the ghost. Carefully unpick the lining, press it and use as the pattern for cutting a new one.

If you're making something in corduroy, remember that while the colour is darker if the nap runs UP, the article of clothing will last longer if the nap runs DOWN.

If you can crochet, you can make superb braid to match your jackets, etc., by using embroidery threads.

Socks can be darned on a sewing machine if there is a free-arm on it, and by using Drima the darn is probably a lot stronger than the sock surrounding it.

If you don't already have one, go and buy a fine, steel crochet hook. Every time you see a loose thread on any garment, use the hook to yoick it to the inside.

Reinforce, reinforce, reinforce. Wherever clothes are likely to wear, spend five minutes when you first get them putting in just a few extra stitches — whether by machine or by hand.

Children's clothes are rarely worn out by one child — they are outgrown first. Therefore, they should be sturdy, but cheap and cheerful. Never spend big money on small people's clothes, unless you have numerous small people to whom they will be handed down.

Have some kind of handy reference for stain removal. Most stains will wash out, but usually quick action is the vital ingredient. Don't spend more on stain removal than the article is worth. Admit defeat and add it to the ragbag or dressing-up box.

If you have corns, you don't need to buy anything to get rid of them, except another pair of shoes which are LARGE ENOUGH. Don't play Cinderella's stepsisters, it only leads to pain.

Colour-coordinated wardrobe? Buy one basic colour and stick to that? When hell freezes over. Why be boring? One of the joys of penny pinching is having lots of clothes for very little money, and if you want an orange outfit, have one. It doesn't HAVE to match anything else in your wardrobe.

Elegance doesn't have to cost pounds. Like beauty and integrity, it comes from within. You really can dress well from charity shops and jumble sales. Stand up straight, hold your head up, and walk tall.

You can actually save money by having a suit made for you by a tailor! How? Have TWO — or even more — pairs of trousers made which will extend the life of the suit several times over. How many times have you reluctantly discarded a perfectly good jacket because the trousers were worn out at the seat?

Buy clothes or fabrics that do not require dry cleaning. Use the dry cleaners only for very best, tailormade suits and high-day-and-holiday wear.

Search around near you to find mill shops, factory outlets and shoe discount stores. Prices are far below those in the high street, and there should be little or no difference in quality.

Well-kept clothes last a lot longer than neglected ones, and look better as well.

For keeping sweaters looking good, there is a wonderful little gadget called D.Fuzz.It which costs a few pence and can usually be found in markets or household shops. These were tucked into Christmas stockings one year and have been treasured ever since!

Hang good clothes up the minute you take them off — but not straight into the wardrobe, let them air in the room first.

If you don't have enough wardrobe space for your clothes, you can make your own multiple-level coat hangers by clipping one hanger over another's neck. Then your clothes won't be crushed so badly.

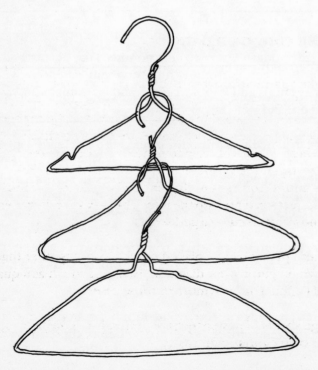

If you are serious about saving money, and say that you can't sew, then learn how to sew!

When you make your own clothes, buy the best quality fabric that you can afford — it will still work out a lot cheaper than buying readymade. You will be pleasantly surprised at the bargains you will find in a mill shop! Name-brand fabrics at a fraction of their high street price.

Even cheaper than buying new fabric is buying good fabric already made up — i.e., jumble sale or charity shop. By buying large sizes or full-gathered skirts you will have a generous amount of fabric to play with, and even if you make a mistake it won't have been an expensive one.

Make your own patterns

You certainly can make your own patterns, and you don't have to take a garment apart to do it. Lay the article of clothing on a large piece of paper — say a roll of wallpaper or brown paper — and pin it down along the seam lines, tracing around the shapes, unpinning as necessary. Sometimes you'll have to make an educated guess as to where a line should go, but when you've taken the garment away, you'll be able to 'join up the dots' and add on a seam allowance. If it looks a bit wonky, don't panic, just straighten up the lines a bit — you're clever enough to know not to cut warped seams.

Pattern pieces can be placed much closer together than shown on cutting-out diagrams, saving as much as a quarter yard (23cm) or even more in some cases.

Large sheets of newspaper are perfectly adequate for making your own clothes patterns.

Multi-size patterns are very useful if you, like most of the other people in this world, are not a standard size. You can choose the measurement that fits YOU. You don't have to cut away the other sizes, either — they may fit someone else in your family. Just cut carefully underneath the pattern — there's rarely more than a 12 mm difference, anyway, between the sizes.

Large envelopes are just right for saving the patterns you've made yourself — a sketch on the outside, title on the top corner.

The '70s and '80s made blue jean cut-offs popular for everyone, but some of us have done it for years, going through several different lengths — remember pedal pushers? Only when their knees wore through did you get Bermuda shorts and finally short shorts.

I can't believe that you don't already do it, but the life of your best shoes can be extended by putting on rubber soles from Woolworths. It is best to put them on before you get a hole in the soles, and some people put them on new soles to stop slips.

Examine your tights to find if there's a particular spot where they always seem to wear, then track down the offending chair/ table/shoe which is snagging them. Fix it.

By all means choose a basic colour for your expensive clothes, but do let yourself relax in cheap and cheerful colours by spending less money on casual clothes.

To keep moths from invading your sweaters, make sure you have them quite clean, then preferably gently steam-iron them, make sure they're absolutely dry, and finally wrap them in newspaper for their summer holiday. If they are very pale in colour, wrap them first in tissue paper or even an old shirt.

Before putting knitted clothes, or even sweatshirt materials, through the washing machine, turn them inside out to prevent 'pilling'. Some are worse than others, but this simple method really works.

You can freshen up suede shoes, gloves, etc., by holding them over the kettle — don't steam your fingers! — and then giving them a brush over.

Clothes and shoes are expensive, so take good care of them. Keep them clean, mended, hang them up to 'rest' after you've worn them, and try to let them rest for a whole day before you wear them again. They will last longer and look better. If you possibly can, alternate your shoes, as well.

To keep your shoes in shape, or to slightly stretch a snug pair, stuff newspaper in them while they're still warm after wearing. And if you are cursed with pongy feet, sprinkle some bicarbonate of soda in with them for a truly refreshing change.

You don't ever have to buy shoe polish. If you have leather shoes, you can polish them with the beeswax-turpentine polish you've made for your furniture — superb for walking boots. Patent leather can be cleaned with vaseline or the inside of a banana skin.

Repair shoes the minute they need it and remember, if high heels get scraped they can often be camouflaged with a felt tip pen.

Is there anything you can't do with vinegar?

Summer fruit and grass stains can often be removed by soaking the garment in vinegar before laundering.

When altering a hemline, dab vinegar on the crease and then iron dry. No telltale line left!

You can even remove chewing gum from your clothes — just use vinegar!

To treat perspiration stains on clothes, soak in a little vinegar water before laundering.

Superb nightshirts can be made by removing the collar (if there is one) from your husband's old school shirts. De-cuff it, and stitch together the sleeve opening. Stitch pre-gathered eyelet edging (broderie Anglaise) all around the neck, cuffs and bottom edges.

You can use a much-loved but perhaps out-of-date shirt or large blouse as a jacket lining.

Most bought interfacings are too stiff, and rarely keep their new appearance; domestic irons just aren't hot enough truly to weld the 'iron-on' ones. Much better interfacing comes from old shirts, or just scraps of cotton/polyester curtain lining fabric, or washed muslin.

The perfect fabric for soft white blouses: curtain lining, cotton/polyester mix. Full stop.

If you have a favourite shirt or blouse which is giving up the ghost, cut it carefully apart and use it as a pattern.!

Men's trousers have an undeserved reputation for being difficult to make. The best pattern, though, is the pair that has fallen apart from having been worn constantly — take them apart, and make educated guesses about where the seam line would have fallen when they were first made.

You can usually rescue a felted sweater. Wash in that wonderful wool cycle, minimum temperature, or wash by hand, and use a fabric rinse with either method. Shake out really hard, stretch like mad, and hang on a big plastic hanger to dry, away from heat. Keep on stretching as it dries, every time you walk past it, stretch the daylights out of it. Do not be tempted to nail it onto a board as in blocking, it seems to be the stretching AS IT DRIES that does the trick.

Children's clothes are so well made that they are outgrown before they become worn out. It is a simple economy to swap clothes between friends and relatives, so that the children always have plenty of clothes and the clothes are put to good use. I am told that the Queen passed clothes down from one child to the next, and if it is good enough for Her Majesty, it is good enough for the rest of us.

Nobody, neither man, woman nor child, needs £60 trainers. Trainers don't need £60 trainers.

Seasonal clothes are cheapest if bought out of season. Anoraks can be bought in the Spring, and swimming trunks in the Autumn. With children it may take some guess-work to judge how big they will be when the time comes to wear them.

Once while on holiday in Scotland there was on the bed a blanket with the date of purchase sewn in. It was dated 1926. Whatever the original price, that was a good buy. Buying quality pays off.

Don't dress up at home. Keep your good clothes for outside occasions, so they look their best. The same goes for shoes.

10
MAKE-UP AND GROOMING

Make your own facial: Use a TINY amount of olive oil to cleanse your face well. Spread the white of an egg (as is or lightly beaten, as you wish) over face and neck. Leave on 15-30 minutes, then rinse off with warm water. Superb.

Make your own smelly-good feely-good bath additives: oatmeal or herbs in a sachet made of old tights, milk straight from the powdered milk box, lemon from the fruit or the bottle.

Bath oil is not beyond the means of the devoted penny pincher — simple but perhaps not sufficiently emulsified to merit a clear bottle. Mix half-and-half cheapest vegetable oil and washing-up liquid. A drop or four of perfume oil if available. It separates, but just shake furiously before each use.

Save all small attractive jars for homemade cosmetics.

Make herb-bags from old tights. Use as a scrub for your bath.

Nail polish lasts longer if kept in the fridge.

Before you throw the used teabags onto the compost heap, you can use them on your eyes as a compress to relieve tiredness. Personally, I think it's the sitting down with eyes closed that does the trick.

If you have percolated coffee, the grounds should either be put onto the compost heap or straight onto garden or pot plant, and you can use them first as a hand scrub, especially after gardening.

Oatmeal really, truly, honestly does make your hands wonderfully soft and smooth. Trust me. Oatmeal soap is a reasonable substitute, but if you could bear squishing your leftover porridge through your hands every day — preferably several times a day — you would be pleasantly surprised at the result!

Read this slowly: you cannot feed your skin from the outside. If you are buying 'nourishing creams' for your skin the only thing you are nourishing is the manufacturer's wallet. If you want to 'feed' your skin cheaply, use something like vegetable oil or egg white, and be aware that if your skin let the stuff inside, it would probably let YOUR inside outside. Your skin may FEEL better if you have creams on it, but it is not being fed by those creams.

Dry lemon and orange peels, pulverise in processor, coffee grinder or mortar and pestle. Keep dry. Add some oil to make face mask. Add a little peel to bicarbonate of soda or soda-and-salt for brushing your teeth.

When you've squeezed out the juice, when you've grated away the peel, there's still life left in that lemon: Pour half a teacup of boiling water onto the lemon skeletons. When cool, remove dead lemons and add 25 g powdered borax and 50 g glycerine, for a lemon hand and body lotion.

Lemon juice makes a super setting lotion. Use it neat. Hair is soft and silky after you brush it.

Make your own lemony shampoo: shave about a bar of soap into a saucepan, cover with water, heat gently until soap melts. If it's thicker than you want, add more water. Add lemon juice.

There is precious little difference between expensive scents and inexpensive ones except the amount of advertising done by the expensive ones.

Baby cream and baby oil are made for the tenderest skin on earth — they are quite suitable for faces of grown-ups as well, and you don't HAVE to own a baby to buy baby products.

If you use cotton wool balls, do make your own from rolls of cotton wool sold at chemists.

Learn to wear gloves. Don't let your hands become chapped and rough in the first place, and you won't need lotions and potions to get them soft and smooth again.

Keep your hands soft and smooth by avoiding expensive cleaners! They are ALL harsh — just check how many have 'rinse hands after use' on the labels. Neither vinegar nor bicarbonate of soda are tough on your skin — quite the contrary.

If you push back your cuticles with your towel as you dry after every bath, you can do without cuticle remover.

Simply massaging your nails helps keep them healthy, and shiny.

Hair care cuts

One really good haircut a year can be cheaper than going to the hairdressers' every few weeks for mediocre cuts. (This applies to women only, sorry chaps — back to the barber, or talk someone near and dear into learning how to cut your hair.)

Grow your hair long. Or learn to cut it yourself. Forget curls unless God gave them to you.

In warm weather, let your hair dry naturally.

Another way of cutting the cost of hair care is to be a model, but I think you have to accept whatever hairdo is being created/practised. Some hairdressers also have certain days on which prices are lower than others.

You will always get gifts at Christmas, so let people know that you actually like perfume oil, or luxurious bath products. It gives them great pleasure to give them to you, and it gives you great pleasure to know that you didn't buy them.

Make your own bath lotions and potions — don't forgo the relaxing pleasure of fun bath products.

A very small container of perfume oil will last for AGES — you only need a few drops in bath water or homemade cosmetics.

You can use half the kitchen cupboard to cleanse the make-up from your face: vegetable oil, mayonnaise, yogurt, lemon juice, egg (yolk, white, both beaten, plain, stirred), smashed-up cucumber, tomato ...

Make lovely little lipstick pots — use tiny little jars from other cosmetic products, or gift jam jars — by gently melting down odds and ends of lipstick and combining with vaseline for your 'designer lip gloss'.

169

There is a wonderful colour consultant: your mirror. Look deep into its eyes and if you like the colour you are wearing, it suits you. Generally, your friends-and-relations will remark on flattering — or ghastly — colours, and they are usually right.

Keep scent bottles securely closed, preferably in their boxes, in a dark place, not sitting prettily on your dressing-table with the sunlight playing on the bottles.

Baby lotion removes make-up.

Loo paper isn't all THAT different from tissues.

You can use lipstick as blusher if you use just a tiny bit.

It's easy to do your own expensive salon hot oil treatment for your hair. Cost: not a lot. Any cooking oil will do it, from cheapest own-brand vegetable oil to gourmet olive. All you have to do is heat the oil to a COMFORTABLE temperature, apply to your scalp and comb through all of your hair. For luxury, wrap your head with a hot towel, leaving essential bits like eyes, nose and mouth free, and leave until you're bored with it or the doorbell rings or about an hour or three go by. Shampoo and rinse.

To avoid having leftover egg yolk when you do the egg white facial, combine your beauty session by having an egg shampoo. Separate the egg, and do your hair first with the egg yolk (trust me, it feels yucky, but it does leave your hair feeling silky) — you can wrap it in a hot towel, or just leave it on for half an hour or so. While the egg is quietly scrambling on your head, apply the white to your face, and then sit and relax for a quarter of an hour. Finally, rinse off the white from your face, and then the yolk from your hair — the latter takes some rinsing to get it all out. Although this whole egg treatment sounds rather unpleasant, it isn't — your hair and skin feel wonderful, and it has cost the price of one egg and a bit of hot water.

The ever versatile vinegar

If you have sensitive skin, you may well find that hair conditioners are an irritant. A money-saving substitute for these — which is much more natural and closer to your skin's pH balance — is vinegar. You only need an ounce or so, diluted if you wish in a mug of water.

You can use vinegar as a deodorant, just wipe on with a cloth. Like bicarbonate of soda, though, it won't stop you perspiring.

To soothe sunburn, you can use vinegar.

Relieve itching skin — anywhere — with vinegar. No need for expensive creams and lotions.

To keep sponges and loofahs fresh, give them an overnight soak in water with a little vinegar, then rinse and let dry.

For an inexpensive and easy mouthwash, use one tablespoon of vinegar in a glass of water. Sprinkle in a spice such as cloves if you like.

Soak pongy socks in 1 part vinegar, 5 parts water before laundering.

If you have athlete's foot, soak your socks in vinegar-water before laundering, and apply neat vinegar to your feet.

If you use shampoo on your hair every day, then your scalp gets hysterical from all the removal of natural oils, and it itches. This makes you use more shampoo. Wonderful for shampoo manufacturers, bad news for scalps.

Herb shampoos, rinses, bath additives, all are yours for virtually free if you have a small herb garden, and you enjoy the beauty of the garden as well, for herbs are most attractive little plants. Easiest of all are simple infusions of herbs with boiling water (not unlike making tea, really). Try camomile for blonde hair, rosemary for brunette, lavender for the bath. You can even use pine needles as a substitute for that expensive one. Lemon juice and beer make wonderful hair rinses.

A most pleasant hand cream is made by mixing rosewater and glycerine. Start with half-and-half, experiment to see what proportions you like best. A drop or four of perfume oil for luxury, but hardly a necessity.

172

The most wonderful lip salve ever and you can make it in no time at all: gently melt a couple of tablespoons of beeswax. Stir in a teaspoon or so of honey, then beat in two to four tablespoons of oil (any kind, cheapest own-brand vegetable is fine). Two spoons will give you a firm product, four a softer one. Pour into tiny jars or pots. This is also the most superb hand cream you will ever come across, and it is suitable for men, women and children.

You can do your own — ouch — waxing of legs with hot beeswax. (This rates right up there with contact lenses: both are possible, but sound too painful even to contemplate — this is definitely for offspring).

If you do make many of your own cosmetics, you might like to know that borax and beeswax in combination are used as emulsifiers (i.e., to keep mixtures from separating). I've never bothered, because it only adds to the cost, and I make them for using, not selling.

Another kitchen ingredient to keep in the medicine cupboard — honey is antiseptic, spread a little over shaving nicks.

One of the more luxurious baths: add a little honey.

If bicarbonate of soda doesn't appeal as a toothpaste, try a little bit of honey — Hippocrates suggested using it on a ball of wool.

Use honey as a face mask — either on its own, or in many, many combinations.

Since you cannot feed your skin from the outside, you can save great amounts of money by not buying nourishing creams, night creams, day creams, vitamin creams and above all wrinkle creams. Never resent growing old, so many are denied the privilege.

Scientists have been unable to discover any difference between expensive lipsticks and the cheap ones.

You can make your own brilliantine! Melt together, in a double boiler, one tablespoon each of vaseline, coconut oil and castor oil, and one teaspoon emulsifying wax. Remove from heat and beat well. The emulsifying wax is to keep it from separating, but you can use beeswax and stir like mad as it cools. A drop of Eau de Cologne wouldn't go amiss.

'Costly thy habit as thy purse can buy'. As true today as when Polonius first uttered the advice to his son, Laertes. Not for nothing does Shakespeare survive.

INDEX

Acorn fittings (plumbing) 62
Agas 58, 143
air bricks 55
air freshening 26, 27, 28
airing cupboard 122
angle iron for tools 82, 101
antifreeze 112
antiperspirant 16, 171
apples 134
appliances 119-27
    faults 119
    instructions 119
    noisy 120
    .seals 120
    wattage needed 123
aprons 81
art and craft materials 33, 83
art gum (as a cleaner) 15
artichokes 97
artificial flowers 50
ashes, fire 58, 93, 103
asparagus 98
athlete's foot 171
attic sales 15
auctions 45

baby 16
    clothes 16, 81
    equipment 81
    food 147
    lotion 167, 170
babysitting circles 22
bacon
    fat 139
    loose 136
bag sealers 124
baked beans 143
baking 11, 120
    paper 39
    powder as substitute for egg 139
banana skins for cleaning 84, 159
bandages 81
bank statements 23
banks 23
barbecue 142
    grills 100, 121
    skewers 87
bargains 40, 42, 46

bath
    additives 165
    cleaners 28
    lotions 169
    oils, making 165, 169
    scrubs 165
bathrooms, moderisation 65
baths 31, 65
batter, for coating 142
batteries, car 112
bay trees 98
beads 51
beans 143
bed-and-breakfasts 23, 115
bed socks 20
bedding 15, 20
beer
    as a hari rinse 72
    as a slug killer 100
    homemade 132, 145
beer bottle as meat tenderiser 132
bees and beekeeping 66-7
beeswax 34, 159, 173, 174
    for leg waxing 173
    polish 69, 70
beetroot 50, 94
bicarbonate of soda 16, 17, 25, 30,
    41, 121, 159, 166, 168, 171, 173
bicycles 115
    maintenance 111
bills, paying 34-5
bird scarers 93, 94
birthday presents 31
biscuit dough, to save 141
biscuits, crisping 142
blackberries 24, 50
blackfly 94
blankets
    binding for 73
    for warmth 20
    old 27
blinds from newspapers 72
blood stains, removal 64
blusher 170
board games 50
boats 115
body lotions, homemade 167
boilers, solid-fuel 57

boiling water 27, 119
bolts, used 66
bonnets, garden 104
bookmarks 84
books 22, 42
  secondhand 71
bookshelves 55
bookshops, secondhand 42, 71
borax 167, 173
borrowing money 32
bottles 13, 17
  as mini greenhouses 94
  as rolling pins 85
  plastic 79, 85
bottle-tops 50
braids, homemade 154
braking, heavy 108
brand names 40, 41
brass polishing 84
bread
  crumbs 134
  freezing 18
  homemade 138
bread bins, cleaning 25
bricks
  air 55, 60
  secondhand 52, 55
brickwork, repointing 70
brilliantine 174
Brillo pads 24
broccoli 136
budgeting 32
building materials 52
building regulations 63
bulbs
  boxes as toy boxes 83
  storage 95
bulk buying 34, 39, 40, 41, 44
bus
  timetables 22
  travel 114
butter 12
  wrapping 140
buttons, saving 15, 80, 151
buying 22, 34, 43

calculator 41, 43
calendar pages 24

camomile 172
candles 11, 85, 87
  ends as firelighters 82
car boot sales 15, 39
card offcuts 83
cardboard boxes 27
  for filing 85
  for storage 33
Carnation milk as substitute for
    cream 133
carpet 64
  cleaning 25, 30
  kitchen 64
  old 63
  stair 64
  underlay 59
  wall-to-wall 30
carrier bags as bin liners 80
carrot fly 97
carrots 97, 131
cars
  batteries 112
  bodywork 112-13
  classic 107
  foreign 107
  four-wheel drive 107
  fuel bills 108
  fuses 111
  heavy 109
  high performance 109
  journeys 113
  maintenance 52, 110-11
  new 107
  oil 109, 111
  radio aerials 87
  rental 108
  secondhand 107, 108, 112
  spare parts 107
  washing 18
cartons (waxed) as firelighters 82
cash purchases 108
casseroles 12
cassette tape as a bird scarer 94
castor sugar, making 140
castor oil 174
cats 127
  discouraging 96
  litter 33

cement 53
  for repointing 70
central heating systems 56, 57
ceramic tiles 49
cereal bags
  for use in freezer 13
  for storage 13
cereal packets 13
  as file-holders 13
  as postcards 13
charity shops 15, 51, 85, 157
cheese
  balls 131
  straws 139
cherries 97
chewing gum, removal of 160
chicken 131
  fat 140
  whole vs pieces 42
chickens, keeping 143
chicory, adding to coffee 135
children 50, 86
  shopping with 40, 44
children's clothing 35, 154, 161
  from remnants 80, 151
chimneys, unused 125
china
  open pattern 39
  saving 11
chocolate, melting 134
Christmas 24, 43
  cards 84
  crackers 73, 74, 83
  decorations 89
  gifts 169
  ornaments 33, 51, 88
  trees 70
  wreath 51
chrome cleaners 113
chutney 133
cinema 22
Citizens' Advice Bureau 23
citrus fruit 11, 18, 21
  peels as firelighters 82
cleaning 15
  cloths 25
  household 25
  materials 16, 24, 28

cleansing liquids 28
cling film 28
cloches 96
clothes 151-62
  drying 122-3
  for messy jobs 73
  homemade 151
  taking care of 156
clothes peg bags 87
clothing
  for patterns 161
  for warmth 19, 20
  protecting 14, 153
  woollen 14
cloves 14
coal 125
  briquettes 125
coat hangers 76, 87
  multiple level 156
coat racks, making 82
cocktail snacks, homemade 131
coconut oil 174
coffee 11
  instant 39
  jars 11
  stretching 135
coffee grounds
  as a hand scrub 165
  for the compost heap 165
  re-using 132
coin purses 40
cold frames, making 101
colour
  choosing paint 54
  coordinating one's clothes 154, 158
complaining about goods 21
compost heaps 79, 82, 95, 101, 103, 104, 165
computers 32
condensation 58
conservatories 63
  blinds for 72
control valves, temperature 56
convenience foods 45, 134
cookbooks 131, 133 see also recipes
cooked meats 136
cookers 19

cooking 12, 19, 120
  fats 140-1
  grease disposal 65
  odours 25
  times 28
cooperative buying 104
corduroy
  as press cloth 80
  sewing with 153
corks, wine 86
corn salad 94
cornflakes 146
  as topping 132
  crisping 132
cornflour as substitute for egg 139
corns (foot) 154
cosmetics, homemade 165, 173
costs
  comparing 42, 43
  knowing 40, 42
cot sheets 81
cotton wool balls 167
coupons 45
courgettes 99
courses 52, 67
craft projects 33, 80
crayons, recycling 83
cream 133
  sour 141
credit and credit cards 31, 41, 43
crisps 41, 146
  homemade 11
crochet hooks 154
crocheting 154
cucumber as a face cleanser 169
cupboards
  changing doors 54-5
  cleaning 25
  painting 55
curtain lining 81
  for blouses 161
curtains
  as dishcloths 86
  as insulation 67, 126
  as tea towels 86
  for clothes peg bags
  closing 20
custard powder as substitute

  for egg 139
cuticle care 168
cutlery trays 14
cut-offs 158
cycle proficiency tests 115

daisies in lawn 100
damp course 60
damsons 50
dandelions 24
darning socks 151
  on a sewing machine 154
decals, removing 73
demolition sites 64
deodorants 16, 17, 171
descaling kettles 26
detergents see washing-up
    liquids
diaries (old) 80
discount outlets 41
dishcloths from curtains 86
dishwashers 119, 121, 122
disinfectant 25
dispensers 28
DIY 22, 49-76
dolls' house furniture 83, 84, 87
donkeys 114
doormats 63
doors
  changing kitchen cupboard 54-5
  closing 20
  flush as work tables 79
  making 55
  secondhand 64
  stripping 68
  using as shelving 55
double glazing 49, 57-8, 60, 126
dowelling, uses 81, 156
drain rods 65
draught
  excluders 60, 126
  prevention 125
drawers 15
  lining 15
dresses (old) 81
dressing up boxes 83, 86, 154
dried beans and peas, softening 147
driving 8, 18

sharing journeys 18
dry cleaning 155
dryers 119, 122
drying clothes 122-3
dusters 24, 25, 81
dusting 84
dyeing 153

earrings 15
Easter eggs 50
eating out 11, 35
egg boxes
    for making decorations 88
    for peat boxes 93
    for storage 33
egg whites 83
    for facials 165
egg yolks, leftovers 135
eggs 12, 83, 139, 142
    for face cleansing 169
    for facials 165
    for shampoos 170
    freezing 143
    shells 95
    substitutes 139
elderberries 24
electric blanket 126
electricity 20-1, 51
    courses 52
    meters 21
    needed for appliances 123
    night-rate 119, 120
    off-peak 57
    wiring 70-1
engine oil, recycled 86
envelopes
    for filing 80, 85
    for saving patterns 158
    making 14
    re-using 87
evaporated milk 131
exercise 11, 19
extension, house 74

fabric
    good quality 157
    non-iron 28
    remnants 80, 85

softening 26
face
    cleaning 169
    masks 166, 173
facials, making your own 165
factory outlets 155
fan belts for cars 111
fans from newspapers 72
fat 140
    clarifying 141
fax machines and faxing 14, 126
felt 49
felt tip pens for repairing high
        heels 159
file-holders 13, 85
fingernail care 168
firelighters 53, 82, 125
fireplaces 125
fires, open 63
floor protection 33
floorboards 66
floors, wooden 30
flour coating for meat 131
flowers
    arrangements 51
    artificial 50
foil
    behind radiators 126
    dishes 82
    kitchen 11, 28
food 131-47
    wastage 22
food bags, re-using 13
fork (table) as a weeder 97
freezers 124
    defrosting 124
    placement 123
freezing
    bread 18
    candles 11
    casseroles 12
    cereal bags for 13
    citrus fruit 18
    vegetables 99
fruit pickers (made from tights) 95
fruit trees 100, 102
fruits 97 *see also* specific fruits
        e.g. lemons, oranges, etc.

fudge 133
fuel 58, 84, 87, 125
fungi 24
furnishings, cleaning 25
furniture 45
    making 55, 67
    polish 69
    removing rings 69
    repairs 49, 67, 68
    stripping 68

games 34, 50
garages 113
garden
    incinerator 103
    labels 97
    machinery 102
    posts 70, 81
    tools 82, 99
    twine 93
gardening 93-104
    clothes 95
gas pilot lights 12
gift tags 84
ginger beer, making 145
globe artichokes 97
gloves 168
    fingerless 20
glue 49, 83
glycerine 167, 172
gorse blossom 50
grape vines 99
grapefruit peels as firelighters 82
grass
    clippings 100
    stain removal 160
gravy, making 135
grease
    bands around trees 100
    disposal 65
greaseproof paper 28, 39
    making 134
greengrocers 44, 83, 84
grooming 165-74
ground elder 99
gutters, house 51

hair
    conditioner 171

drying 168
human 82
rinses 172
haircuts 168
ham, cooking 134
hand
    care 168
    creams 28, 166, 167, 172, 173
    scrubs 165
handkerchiefs 81
handles, re-using 86
hanging baskets 95
hats 20
    paper 73
heaters, multifuel 126
heating 19, 20, 29, 56-7, 63
    central 56, 124, 125
    control 124-5
    oven 120
    saving 58
hedges 103
    hawthorn 102
hemline creases, removal of 160
herb-bags 165
herbs 28, 100, 147, 172
    as a bath additive 165, 172
high heels, repairing 159
hoeing 99
holes in pockets 153
home-tune mechanic 111
honey 27
    as an antiseptic 173
    as a bath additive 173
    as a face mask 173
    as a sugar substitute 140
    cooking with 140
hops 147
horseradish 98
horses 86
hot oil treatment 170
hot toddies,, making 27
hot water
    bottles 126
    pipes 56
    tanks 58, 59
hotels 23
house
    extensions 74

gutters 51
  moves 34, 62-3
  protection 24
humour, sense of 29

ice cream from leftovers 132
ice cube trays 15
icing sugar 140
incinerator, garden 103
income 22
initials 80
insulation
  curtains as 67
  house 56
  hot water tanks 58, 59
  loft 59
interest and interest rates 32
interfacings 161
interlining scraps 80
irons and ironing 14, 19, 123, 158
itching, relief from 171

jacket linings, replacing 153, 161
jam making 138
  from stewed fruit 137
jars
  as mini greenhouses 94
  weight and size 43
jewellery, old 83
joints, furniture 67
journeys, car 113
juice 12
jumble sales 15, 39, 51, 95, 151, 157
jump leads 111
junk food, homemade 131
junk mail 14, 85

kettles 27
  descaling 26
keys as toys 83
kitchen cupboards 54-5
knitted clothes, preventing
    pilling 159
knitting needle end corks 86
knobs (door, bed, etc.) 82, 86

labels 44
lamb's lettuce 94

lampshades, making
  from maps 80
  from newspapers 73
land clearance 103
laundry economics 122-3
lavatory cisterns 62
lavender 28, 100, 153, 172
lawns 100
  mowers 102
  feed 100
leather
  belts 86
  washers 86
leaves as compost 103
leg waxing 173
lemon thyme 100
lemons 11, 26, 27, 51, 167
  adding rinds to sugar 137
  for face cleansing 169
  for a hand lotion 167
  freezing bits 18
  juice as bath additive 165
  juice as hair rinse 172
  peels as firelighters 82
  peels as a face mask 166
letters 28, 32
lettuces
  cooked 136
  keeping fresh 136
  planting 18, 94
libraries 22, 42, 131, 133
light bulbs 20
lights 21
lipbrushes 18
lip salves 173
lipstick 18, 121, 169, 170, 174
  cases 80
liquidiser 140
lobbies 58
lofts 59
log-roller 125
long distance calls 19
loo rolls 40, 170
loofahs, freshening 171
lovage 100
lunch bags 146
lunches
  packed 11

school 145

magazines
  buying 32, 54
  uses 82
maintenance, importance of 29
make-up 17, 18, 165-74
manure 102, 103, 104
maps as wallpaper 73
marble, cleaning 26, 51
margarine 12
  wrapping paper 140
markets 42
Marmite sticks 131
marrows 99
materials 63, 151
mayonnaise for face cleansing 169
meals, cheap 31
meat loaf leftovers 133
meats
  cheap cuts 31, 131
  eating 141
  tenderiser 132
mending 153
menu planning 131
metric conversions (in piping) 61
microwaves 121
mileage, car 113
milk 12, 139
  as a bath additive 165
  evaporated 131
  tinned and dried 141
mill shops 155, 157
mint (garden) 99
modernisation 65
moles 95
money 23, 24, 29
moss
  for hanging baskets 95
  in lawns 100
moths, killing 14, 158
mould prevention 25
mouthwashes 171
muesli 132
mulch 102
multifuel heaters 126
mushrooms 24, 131
music centres as propagators 82

nail polish 165
nails
  reclaimed 52
  straightening 66
nappies 16
necklaces 51
needlepoint lace bases 84
'needs' 32
net contents weight 43
newspapers 72-3
  as art and craft materials 33
  as carpet underlay 59
  as cat litter 33
  as firelighters 82, 125
  as floor protection 33
  as fuel 58, 87, 125
  as paper towel 146
  as sunshade for plants 103
  as wallpaper 73
  as wrapping paper 3
  for blinds 72
  for cleaning chrome 113
  for cleaning oven shelves 121
  for clothing patterns 157
  for compost heap 104
  for conservatory blinds 72
  for fans 72
  for games 343
  for horse's stables 86
  for lampshades 73
  for paper hats 73
  for placemats 72
  for shoe insoles 151
  for stretching shoes 159
  for window cleaning 26
  for wrapping things in 33, 34
  in salad drawers 133
  in unused chimneys 125
  logs 125
nightcaps 20
nightshirts, making 160
notebooks, spiral (prices of) 39
nuts
  for wood colour restoration 70
  oats as substitute for 136
  shells for mulch 102
nylon scourers 24, 26

oatcakes, homemade 133
oatmeal
  as bath additive 165
  as hand cream 166
oats 112, 136
olive oil 12
onions
  storage 136
  to discourage cats 96
orange boxes 84
orange squash, homemade 142
oranges 14, 18
  adding rinds to sugar 37
  peels as firelighters 82
  peels for a face mask 166
organising 14, 15
outlet shops 41, 42
ovens
  cleaning 121
  shelves, cleaning 121
  timed 31
overdrafts 23
own-brands 39, 40

packed lunches 11
paint 53-4
  choice of colour 54
  mixing 53
  storing 53, 54
  stripping 68
paintbrushes 53
  as firelighters 53
  cleaning 53
painting 76
  walls 49
paintings 31
paper
  hats 73
  lining 15, 33
  making 88
  scrap 14
  saving 32
  towels 30, 146
  wallpaper 15
  washable 15
  wrapping 24, 33, 83
  writing 14, 28
papier mâché 72

parsley 94, 100
pasta 133, 139
  dough, to save 141
paste 49
pastry 139
  to save 141
patchwork quilts 80, 85
pâté, making 142
patent leather, cleaning 84, 159
patterns, clothes 161
  making your own 157
  multi-size patterns 158
paying bills 34-5
pears 97
peas 133
peat 103
  boxes 93
pepper to discourage cats 96
perfume 18, 169
  bottles 15
perspiration stains, removal of 160
pests (garden) 97, 100, 103
pesticides 97
petrol 18, 45, 109
  consumption 108, 109
pets 27, 143
photographs 14
  backing 84
pickle-making 133
pigeons 141
pilling, prevention 159
pillow cases 81
pine
  cones 28
  needles 172
placemats
  from magazines 82
  from newspapers 73
plant ties 96
plants 96
  wild edible 24
plastering 52
plastic bottles
  as mini greenhouses 94, 96
  as moulds 85, 87
  as scoopers 79
plastic containers as toys 83
plastic labels 97

plastic net bags 79
plastic, repairing 74
plastic sheeting 49, 58, 75
    to kill weeds 103
'plastic wood' 49
play dough 49
plumbing 52, 60-2
polish, furniture 69
polystyrene sheeting 58
polythene bags 19
pomanders 14
porches 58, 59
pork 131
    belly 142
porridge oats (to stop car radiator
    leaks) 112
postcards 13, 14
    making 84
postage and posting 14, 23, 32, 46
posters (election) 75
potatoes 41, 147
potting-up pots 94
pot-pourri sachets 81
press cloth 80
pressure cookers 120
prices
    comparing 42, 43
    knowing 40, 42
prints 71
propagators 82
purses 40

quarry tiles 26
quilting frame from dowelling 81
quilts 23
    making 80
quinces 97
quizzes for Christmas crackers 83

rabbits 141
radiators 57
    bleeding 57
    car 111, 112
    foil behind 126
    individual controls 125
radio 22
rag rugs 55, 73
rags for making paper 88

Rayburns 58, 143
razor blades 17
reading 21, 22
recipes
    file cards 84
    storage 32
record cleaner 83
recycling 79-89
redecoration 75
refrigeration 139
refrigerators 124, 139
    placement of 123
repairs 49
repointing brickwork 70
re-upholstery 67
rhubarb 93
ribbon 81
rice 133, 136
riddles for Christmas crackers 83
rings, removing from furniture 69
rolling pins from bottles 85
roof-racks 113
roofs 59
    flat 70
    heat loss from 59
    slates 71
    tiles 56
rosehips 24
rosemary 28, 100, 142, 172
roses 95
rosewater 172
rotavator 102
rubber bands 26, 79
rubber gloves 26, 79, 84
rubber sink taps 11
rugs 64
    making 55, 73
rust on cars 112-13

sage 100, 142
salads
    early 94
    leftover 135
salt
    as a weedkiller 101
    for teeth cleaning 17, 166
    pillow for earache 126
sandpaper sponge 68

sauce bottles 13, 134
saucepans 120
sausages
  cooking 139
  homemade 136
saving 43
sawdust 49
scent 167
  bottles 15, 170
school lunches 145
scoopers, making 79
scourers 24
  making 79
  nonscratch 86
scouring powder 12
scrap
  cards 84
  equipment 66
  material 85, 151
  paper 14
  wood 49
screws 66, 75
seasonal clothes, buying 162
secondhand
  bookshops 42, 71
  items 45
  tools 71
seeds
  lettuce 18
  saving your own 96
setting lotion, homemade 167
sewing 157
sewing tables 79
shampoo 17, 28, 171
  egg 170
  herb 172
  homemade 167
sheets 15
  binding for 73
  for curtain lining 81
  for pillow cases 81
shoes 30, 41
  alternating 158
  discount shops 155
  getting rid of smells 159
  leather 86
  maintaining 159
  making from interlining 80

outdoor 30, 159
  polish 159
  repairs 151
  re-soling 158
  stretching 159
shopping 39-45
  lists 39, 45
  when hungry 39
shops
  alternate 40, 42
  map 41
shower doors, cleaning 25
showers 31
shrubs as wind breaks 59
silicone baking paper 39
sink taps 11
sketching 21
skimmers from tights 95
skin care 166
skirts 20
slates 71
sleeping 20
sloes 24
slow-cookers 31
slug killers 100
small ads 45
smoking 21
  giving up 34
snail traps 100-1
soap
  to keep your nails clean 96
  to make 88
  to make last longer 18, 34
socks 20
  deodorising 171
  for dusting 84
soft fruit 97
sorrel 24, 99
sound-proofing 57
soups 135, 136, 143
sour cream, making 141
soya beans 13
soya flour as egg substitute 139
spatula, plastic 39
special offers 43, 44, 46
spending
  patterns 31
  record keeping 22

spinach 50, 94, 99
sponges 24, 28
    freshening 171
'sprout' sprouts 93
stain removal 154
stair carpets 64
stamps 46
staples (food) 45
steam ironing woollens 14, 158
steamers 120-1
steaming food 132
stick-on labels 85
stiletto heels 153
stockings (old) 26, 96
    as fan belts 111
    as nylon scourers 26
    as strainer 84
    as stuffing for toys 50
    to make fruit picker 95
    to make twine 85, 96
stone, cleaning 26
storage
    jars 11
    packets 13
stoves, free-standing 63
strainers, from old tights 84
strawberries 44
string 81
stripping wood and furniture 68
stuffing 81
suede, cleaning and freshening
    15, 159
sugar 137, 140
    substitutes 140
suits, tailormade 155
sunburn, easing 171
supermarkets 44, 46
swapping
    plants 95
    services 21
sweaters 19, 20
    felted 161
    old 27
    taking care of 156, 158
sweatshirts, preventing pilling 158
sweetcorn 97, 99
sweets 40

T-shirts 153
table napkins 28
talcum boxes 15
tansy 100
tape as a bird scarer 94
taps, sink 11, 60, 61, 62
tea 11, 95, 134
    as food for plants 95
    bags 165
    leaves 95, 134
tea towels from curtains 86
teeth cleaning 17, 166
telephoning 19, 21, 126
    long distance calls 19
temperature control valves 56, 125
tenderising meat 147
thermal insoles 151
thermal underwear 151
    from tights 153
thermostats 57, 125
thread spools 84, 151
tights 15, 20
    as fan belts 111
    as nylon scourer 26
    as plant ties 96
    as strainer 84
    as stuffing for toys 50
    for drying herbs 147, 153
    for making thermal underwear
        153
    making last longer 152
    preventing snagging 151, 158
    thick 152
    to make a fruit picker 95
    to make twine 85
    washing 152, 153
tiles
    ceramic 49
    cleaning 25, 26
    quarry 26
    secondhand 64
timber see wood
timetables, bus and train 22
tins
    for steaming food 132
    tightly-closing 83
    weights and size 43
toadstools 24

tobacco, growing 103
toddy, hot 27
toffee 13
tomatoes 133
   for face cleansing 169
   freezing 134, 137
   homegrown 137
   storing 137
tools 63, 71
   gadunger 101
   garden 82, 101
   lending 75
   old 39
   paintbrushes 53
   secondhand 71
toothbrushes for cleaning 29
toothpaste 17, 173
towels 15, 19
   as washcloths 85
   binding for 73
   getting rid of smells in 123
   tea 86
towing brackets 113
toy box 83
toy circle 82
toys 50, 83
   from dowelling 81
   from tins 83
   stuffing for 50
train
   timetables 22
   travel 114-15
trainers 162
transport 107-15
travelling abroad 113
trays, ice cube 15
trees as wind breaks 59
trips, car 113
trousers, making 161
Tube travel 114
turkey 147
turnips 49
TV 21, 22, 31
twine
   garden 93
   made from old tights 85
tyres 110
   pressure 110, 111
   spare 110

underground travel 114
underwear 19, 25
   making 88
upholstery 67

vacuum flasks
   cleaning 26
   for saving hot water 121
   for yogurt making 140
vacuum cleaners 119
vanilla beans with sugar 137
vaseline 169, 174
   as a shoe polish 159
vegetable dyes 153
vegetables 44, 51
   peelings 79
   planting 93
vegetarians 141
velvet
   as press cloth 80
   for record cleaining 83
videos 22
vinegar 25-6, 51, 168
   as deodorant 171
   as hair conditioner 171
   as mouth wash 171
   as substitute for egg 139
   as substitute for wine in
      cooking 147
   for athlete's foot 171
   for cleaning chrome 113
   for cleaning grass and fruit
      stains 160
   for erasing hemline creases 160
   for making sour cream 141
   for removing chewing gum 160
   for removing decals 73
   for removing perspiration
      stains 160
   for washing clothes 122, 123, 171
   in cooking 147
   to keep sponges and loofahs
      fresh 171
   to relieve itching 171
   to soothe sunburn 171
vines, grape 99

visual brighteners 46

walking 18, 24, 115
wallpaper 15
  cartoons as 73
  for making clothes patterns 157
  newspaper as 73
wallpapering 49
washable paper 15
washcloths from towels 85
washers (taps) 61, 66
washing
  car 113
  clothes 122
  hand 19
  machines 122, 123
  powder 19, 46, 122
washing-up bowls 29
washing-up liquid 12, 13, 17,
    27, 28, 30
  as pesticide 97
  on carpets 30
wastepaper bin liners 80
water 12
  as an extender 12
  boiling 18, 27, 119, 121
  butts 95
  cold 19, 20
  draining systems 62
  heaters 125
  hot 19, 20, 29
  tanks 62
  warm (almost free) 12
  washing up 97
water biscuits, homemade 133
water pipes
  dripping 60
  frozen 59
  repairs 61
wax, emulsifying 174
wedding 50
  cake 50
weeders 97
weedkillers 97, 101
weeds, killing 18, 103
white spirit 81
wind breaks 59
windows

as cold frames 101
cleaning 26
replacement 60, 65
secondhand 64
window-shopping 41
wine 42
  corks 86
  homemade 144-5
wire (coat hangers as) 101
wiring (electrical) 70-1
women as penny pinchers 35
wood
  free 125
  reclaimed 66, 68
  rotting 66
  scrap 49, 52, 55
  secondhand 64, 68
  stripping 68
wood-burning stoves 58, 87
wooden boxes 55, 84
wooden pallets 52, 101
woodworm 69
wool
  cycles on machine 122, 161
  for good twine 93
  for warmth 20
  recycled 85
woollen clothing 14, 158
  cleaning 122
work clothes 95
work tables 79
working, part-time 27
wrapping paper 24, 33
  storing 83
wrench, adjustable 71
writing 13, 21, 28

yarn scraps 80
yeast extract 12
Yellow Pages 46, 66
yogurt
  for face cleansing 169
  making 140
yogurt pots
  as potting-up pots 94
  label sticks from 97

zips, saving 80